Babu Purna Chandra Mukharji

Report on the Excavations on the Ancient Sites of Pataliputra in 1896-97

Babu Purna Chandra Mukharji

Report on the Excavations on the Ancient Sites of Pataliputra in 1896-97

ISBN/EAN: 9783337384814

Printed in Europe, USA, Canada, Australia, Japan

Cover: Foto ©ninafisch / pixelio.de

More available books at **www.hansebooks.com**

A REPORT

ON THE

EXCAVATIONS ON THE ANCIENT SITES OF PÁTALIPUTRA

(PATNA-BANKIPUR)

IN

1896-97.

ILLUSTRATED BY 58 PLATES.

By

BABU PURNA CHANDRA MUKHARJI,
Archæologist.

An Illustrated Report on the Excavations on the sites of Pátaliputra in 1896-97.

INDEX.

LIST OF PLATES.

An Illustrated Report on the Excavations on the sites of Pataliputra in 1896-97.

INTRODUCTION

At the end of the last century, when Sir William Jones discovered rather wrongly the identity of Sandrocottus with Chandragupta, the founder of the Maurya dynasty, the site of Palibothra was sought for in different directions. And, though some held that Patna might be the proper place, others attempted to find it elsewhere. D'Anville, for example, located it at Allahabad; Major Rennel, at Kanauj; Wilford, at some distance north of Rajmahal; while Franklin, in a special pamphlet, endeavoured to show that it was at Bhagalpur, as if Champa and Pataliputra were one. They did not then know of the local tradition of the Brahmans and the Jainas, which is not yet forgotten. Even though the Pandits informed Dr. Buchanan in about 1810 (Martin's "Eastern India," volume I), Major Rennel adhered to the opinion that it was at the old junction of the Kosi with the Ganges, near Rajmahal, as at first proposed by Major Wilford in "Asiatic Researches," volume V. But the solution of the question was found so unsatisfactory and uncertain that the attempt of identification was given up till 1876, when General Cunningham deputed Mr. Beglar to trace the city and the Son.

As to the ancient course of the river Son, Ravenshaw had proved it to be in the Bengal Asiatic Society's Journal, Volume XIV, page 137, and Lieutenant Maxwell traced its ancient bed from [illegible] to just west of Bankipore, where it joined the Ganges. Rennel also found that the Son flowed further eastward and south of Patna joining the Ganges near Fatwa. Mr. Beglar, however, assumed that Erannoboas (Sanskrit, Hiranyavaha) was the Gandak, and proved afresh that the Son joined the Ganges at Patna. But he located the ancient city north of the present town, which was, he supposed, eaten away by the river, it having changed its course considerably southward long before the Muhammadan invasion.

In 1877-78, General Cunningham visited Patna, and, generally agreeing with Mr. Beglar, concluded that about half a mile of the breadth of the ancient city, which was originally one-and-a-half miles, "may have been swept away by the Ganges." But in identifying the lost monuments, mentioned by the Chinese pilgrims, he grouped them too close to one another at the [illegible] village of [illegible].

In April 1892, Dr. Waddell re-opened the question of the identification of the ancient monuments of Pataliputra, and utilising the [illegible] of the Chinese records by the pilgrims, wrote, in his pamphlet on the Classic Capital of Asoka, that "having lately had an opportunity of visiting Patna, I explored its neighbourhood and was surprised to find that not only was the site of Pataliputra preserved practically unencroached by the Ganges, but that all the chief landmarks of Asoka's palace, monasteries, and monuments remained so patent, that in the brief space of one day I was able to identify most of them by taking Hiuen Tsiang's accounts as my guide." His results were very valuable, which would have been far better, had he consulted Fa Hian also.

On the publication of his monograph entitled "Asoka's Classic Capital," Government was induced to order excavations. The Trustees of the Indian Museum, where I was attached at the time, recommended that I should be put in charge. But shortly after, they changed their mind in favour of Dr. Führer of the Lucknow Museum, who, in 1895, and with a grant of Rs. 1,000, excavated the two stupas at Pahari without any successful results. Dr. Waddell thereupon wrote on 25th February 1895, that "I am sorry to find that Government has been so ill-advised as to have undertaken such destructive and costly excavations at a place which was the least likely place to yield useful results. It seems almost incredible that any one who had studied the descriptive accounts of the Chinese pilgrims, and who had visited the spot with my preliminary report in hand, as Mr. Führer admits having done, should not observe at a glance that the Panch Pahari or Five Pahari [illegible] from the debris of the Maurya palace, or would be other than the five Stupas, as identified by me.... These excavations, laborious as they have been, have cleared out hundreds of cubic yards of bricks and brick-debris, and have left a yawning chasm 40 feet deep, which is so dangerous to the public, that the Magistrate proposes to fill it up again at a further cost of Rs. 700."

The Indian [illegible] then recommended further excavations by some competent agency, and Mr. Mills, the Inspector of works, consented to supervise. Rs. 5,000 was again sanctioned, and in March 1896 digging was commenced, at Kumrahar, Bulandibagh, and Rampur. Certain interesting relics were obtained, and an important discovery was made at the last place, but the Public Works Department agency did not prove successful. And Mr. Mills leaving, Mr. [illegible], the Secretary, [illegible] an expert, Government deputed me to the work on 7th December 1896. A further grant of Rs. 3,000 was asked for, of which Rs. 2,500 was sanctioned. Since Mr. Mills was shortly after sent to famine relief works, I at first followed the instructions given by Dr. Waddell, and accordingly commenced work at Kumrahar and its neighbourhood. After a few trial diggings, I gave up Bulandibagh and [illegible] as not very promising.

In addition to the above-mentioned three places, Dr. Waddell wanted me to excavate the following places, namely, Jamuna Ghat and the villages around, Bahadurpur, [illegible], [illegible], [illegible], [illegible] and [illegible], the [illegible] mounds on the north of the railway, Chhoti and Bari Pahari, Bhikhnapahari, the mounds at [illegible], [illegible], and Mangles' Tank, and the several sites of the ancient town precincts of Pataliputra. Of these places, I worked at Jamuna Ark and Kumrahar and its neighbourhood, which yielded remains of brick structures and the fragments of a large Asoka pillar and others. Near Ali Khan's tank and the railway, near Sewaicon, I discovered a series of very important piles, presumably on the south bank of the ancient bed of the Son, about 15 feet below the present ground level. These works occupied my attention till the 10th of March, when I was deputed to the Terai of the Champaran district to search for Kusinagara, the last site of the death of the Buddha. In the Terai I brought to light a number of ancient ruins, and it struck me as extremely probable that Kusinagara was at Lauriya, where I discovered that Nandangarh (General Cunningham's Navandgarh) represents the biggest brick stupa in India.

Returning to Bankipore on the 4th April, I resumed excavations at Kumrahar, Narainpur, Bahadurpur, Rampur, Bhikhnapahari, and Lohanipur. At these places I discovered several remains of Maurya architecture and arts, which I followed up till the second week of June, when the rains stopped all my outdoor works. And, though I have succeeded in tracing the colonnade of the palace, and the pillar of Asoka at Kumrahar, and the Sun pillars at Sewaicon, two other Maurya pillars with Buddhistic railings and other remains at Lohanipur, the wooden palisades with moats at several places, and brick buildings underneath the big mound of Bhikhnapahari, still many more sites remain to be probed into within and without the great city, in order to complete the results of excavations on a scientific basis.

In connection with the identification of the sites of Pataliputra, in which I find myself differing from Dr. Waddell, an epigraphical scholar, I beg to submit that Nandangarh, which I propose to identify with the Pasanadi stupa; Chhoti Pahari, the fort of Chanakya, Chandragupta's tutor and minister, and other important sites visited by the Buddha and the Chinese pilgrims, need be excavated. For, without determining the positions of such places as Swetadwipa, the two stupas of Ananda on both sides of the Ganges, the value of the different sites of Pataliputra cannot be properly understood. Dr. Waddell while going on furlough, wrote to me early in April last that I should "stick close to Hiuen Tsiang's account. It is only the fort and its immediate surroundings that you should excavate, and I hope your excavations at Narainpur may be continued speedily, and that you may find really interesting and important remains." I should, in fact, study all Buddhistic places, by survey and excavation, taking Pataliputra and Vaisali as centres.

As to the results of my works already achieved as economically as I could, I beg to submit that important facts have been brought to light. (1) The first is that Pataliputra stood between 10 and 15 feet below the present level of the ground. (2) Some of the important and sacred places visited by the Chinese pilgrims have been identified with some degree of certainty. (3) The wooden palisade of Palibothra, visited by Megasthenes in about 310 B.C., has been traced to a certain extent. (4) Several peculiarities of the Maurya architecture, which does not show any Greek influence, have been noted. (5) The arts and sculptures of that age also yield some interesting features in the ornaments and beads; and an important fact, that glass was manufactured in those days, has apparently surprised all visitors by my collection of ancient relics. (6) The ancient coins found in my excavations were of several types, ranging from the Punch-marked to the Gupta, and some later, which proves Mr. Smith's theory that Pataliputra ceased to be the capital of the Magadha empire after the conquest of Western India by Chandragupta II. And, in compiling the history of Pataliputra, written in connection with this report, I have made (7) the greatest of my discoveries, namely, that the Greek Sandrokottos was not Chandragupta, the founder of the Maurya dynasty, but Asoka the Great himself, who mentions Alexander and his generals, latterly independent kings, in his inscriptions. (8) The last point I beg to bring to prominent notice is that Pataliputra decayed in the 7th century A.D., which fact, with the fate of Vaisali, disproves the theory of modern scholars that all productions of the so-called latter arts, as also inscriptions in archaic *Devanagari*, should be relegated to the tenth century A.D. or thereabouts.

I beg at the same time to submit that, though I have taken the utmost care in compiling the historical account, and consulted all available authorities on the subject, I am personally responsible for my opinions. Tentative theories possess a certain value, for, while temporarily explaining problems otherwise inexplicable, they ultimately lead to the truth, when the true cause for their being given up. General Cunningham's theory of Kasia being the site of the Buddha's Parinirvana served its purpose in its time. And I would have most probably missed the discovery of the big stupa at Nandangarh, Lauriya, had I not formed the theory of this being the site of Kusinagara at Lauriyah.

In conclusion, I beg to acknowledge with thanks the interest that Mr. [illegible] and Dr. Waddell took in advising and instructing me in my works of excavation. On their going away, the former on famine deputation and the latter on furlough, I have been very fortunate to find in Mr. Bourdillon, the Commissioner, a most sympathetic officer, who, though extremely busy with famine matters, spared time to see my works. It is due to his kind encouragement, that made me bold to make new explorations, bringing to light important monuments at Lohanipur, Bahadurpur, Kumrahar and elsewhere. And I am especially grateful to him for the important results that I have achieved in my historical investigations. I should also thank Mr. V. A. Smith* of Gorakhpur, an authority in ancient coins and antiquities, who was so good as to decipher the Gupta coins I found here, and to check the identifications that I, differing from Dr. Waddell, propose to make of the ancient sites at Pataliputra, and generally to help me in different ways.

P. C. Mukherji,

Archaeologist.

* Now Chief Secretary to the Government of N.-W. P. and Oudh.

CHAPTER I.—HISTORY OF PATALIPUTRA.

Pre-Buddhist Pataligama.

Before the rise of Pataliputra, there was a pre-historic town, by name Pushpapura or Kusumapura, literally the Town of Flowers, so called because the King's palace was said to have been ornamented with many flowers [illegible], about which a tradition is recorded by Hiuen Tsiang in 637 A.D., who tells that at that primitive time the age of men was of "incalculable length." Afterwards, when their lives extended to "a few thousand years" (which we can safely read as about one hundred years), the town was called Pataliputra, the Pataligrama* of the Buddha's time, after a *Patali* tree, the trumpet-flower tree. The legend was that the spirit of this tree gave her daughter in marriage to a young man, once a recluse, for whom she built a house in the suburbs of Kusumapura. Dr. Buchanan Hamilton also records a local tradition that Sudarsan Raja, probably eighteenth in [illegible] descent from Maga, conferred the town on his daughter, Patali, who enlarged it like a city, and hence called it Pataliputra, and who dedicated a temple to Patana Devi, the presiding goddess of the town. The antiquity of this town, which, according to tradition, was founded by [illegible], the brother of Krishna, [illegible] B.C., must therefore be very great.

* Patana was probably a village name of the tree [illegible]

The critical explanation of the legend appears to be that a citizen from Kusumapura built, after cutting a neighbouring forest, a garden-house near a *Patali* tree, under which there was, as we generally see now, a rude representation of a sylvan deity, the archetype of Patana Devi, where a fair was periodically celebrated by the inhabitants. In course of time, this suburb increased in importance, and a small village, Pataligrama, grew in association with the legend of the *Patali* tree, for the original builder of the garden-house was only remembered by the ignorant villagers as no other than the son or son-in-law of the spirit of the tree. Afterwards, when the rivers inundated and ruined Kusumapura, Pataliputra became its natural successor. The levels of the different localities in those days, as now, were not uniform; at one geological period, the Ganges raised its banks higher than the Punpun and the Son, and at another, the Punpun or the Son, or both together, attained greater eminence. The accumulation of the silt, owing to the annual inundations, occurred at one period at a certain area northward, at other times at other places southward. The ruins of Pataliputra are at present imbedded between 10 and 20 feet below the present level of the ground.

The Buddha at Pataligrama in [illegible] B.C.

At the time of the Buddha, Pataligrama appears to have been a large village, ruled by a Brahman of great learning, an overseer of Magadha, who, as recorded in *Maha-Pari-Nirvana-Sutra*, used to observe the omens of the land, somewhat like the Meteorological Department of our day. The [illegible] *Avadana* states that the inhabitants of this village suffered great hardships and vexations by being turned out of their houses for a fortnight or a month at a time to accommodate the officers and messengers of the two kingdoms, Magadha and Vaisali, who were continually passing and repassing between Rajgriha and Vaisali. They had, therefore, to build a rest-house, called *Chaitya* in some versions, in the middle of the village. The lay devotees of the Buddha invited him, while he was going from Rajagriha to [illegible], to this chaitya hall, of which the floor was covered with sand and spread with mats. They also prepared a water-pot and an oil lamp. The Buddha with his alms bowl and [illegible], went there in the forenoon and washing his feet and facing the east, took his seat against the central post, which, as one can read [illegible] the floor, shows the structure to be lofty and wooden, and having [illegible]. His disciples occupied the western portion of the chaitya, being seated at his back, while the lay-devotees of Pataligrama, fronting the saint, sat on the eastern half, when the Buddha gave a sermon on the fivefold gain of righteousness and the fivefold loss for want of it, far into the night. Dismissing his hearers, he then went to a [illegible], an unoccupied room for meditation. At dawn he saw with his divine eye the powerful genii who lead the hearts of kings and ministers to build dwelling places. At this time, Sunidha and Vassakara were, at the command of King Ajatasatru, constructing a fortified town (*Nagara*), ultimately to conquer the neighbouring Vajjis of Vaisali. The saint praised their skill, and prophesied that as far as Aryan people dwell, as far as merchants travel, this would become the chief city, one hundred years after his *Parinirvana*, being [illegible] by high [illegible] and having [illegible] with [illegible] fire, water, and internal dissensions. The two ministers invited him to dine at their house. The Buddha after attending the invitation, departed out of the new town by the eastern gate, which the ministers christened the Gotama gate. The Ganges was then over-flowing; and his disciples began to seek for boats, rafts of wood and wicker basket-work, when the saint miraculously crossed over to the opposite bank with his 1,250 disciples and went to [illegible], on his way to Vaisali. The place where he crossed was since known as Gotama's ferry.

The first fort built by Ajatasatru.

Pataliputra's buildings in [illegible] B.C.

Three years after the death of the saint, Ajatasatru conquered Vaisali from this Nagara, which had been constructed for that purpose. According to the *Vishnu*, *Vayu* and other *Puranas*, it was Udayasva, the son of Ajatasatru, who founded Pataliputra in 519 B.C., by which I understand that he completed the work commenced by his father. According to the Jaina chronicles, recorded in the *Parisista* parvan, Udaya, succeeding his father Kunika at Champa, which was founded by the latter, sought an auspicious site [illegible] a magnificent Patali tree and on the bank of the Ganges, where was found the skull of a famous Jaina saint. The artisans of the king, arriving at the spot, went round the tree in an ever-widening circle, till they heard the cry of a jackal. They then stopped the measuring thread, and thus marking the limit of the new capital, raised a fine Jaina temple in the centre, as also many other stately buildings for the king, who was a devout Jaina. Here he was assassinated by the son of a king from Ujjain, who had been dethroned by Udayin.—*Jacobi's Parisishta*, page 14. According to *Asoka[illegible] Vidana*, King Munda, who killed his father Udayi, lived at Pataliputra. He was probably referred to in the Tibetan accounts (Dulva) as King Ajatasatru, who obtained one-half of the relics of Ananda, the third patriarch of the Buddhistic Church, built a chaitya in the city of Pataliputra in about 60 A.B. In 65 A.B. the nobles of Rajagriha or as some say of Pataliputra, put an end to the patricide dynasty, and elected Sisunaga of Benares as king.

Udayin leaving no heirs, as the Jains say, the nobles elected Nanda as his successor and king in 60 A.V. (467 B.C.). This Nanda appears to be Nandivardhana, the King of Champaran, who was said by Jacobi's[illegible] to be a beautiful son by a barber. Now 467 B.C. falls in the reign of Sisunaga of the Buddhistic chronicles, who is evidently the Nandivardhana of the Puranas, and [illegible] of the 3 [illegible], the King of Champaran (Champaran of the present day), who is said by Taranath, the Tibetan historian, to have conquered Magadha from a Brahman king. According to the *Puranas*, the duration of the Nanda dynasty was 100 years, which figure we get by subtracting 320 B.C., the commencement of Chandragupta's reign, from 420 B.C., that of Sisunaga. The identity of Nanda with Nandi, Nanda, and Sisunaga therefore, becomes evident. The genealogy of the Nandas appears to be as shown below from the *Puranas*:—

Sisunaga, Nanda or Nandi.

Kakavarna, Kalasoka or Mahapadma.

Nine Nandas by Queen [illegible]. Chandragupta of Mura.

In 453 B.C., Kalasoka succeeded his father and removed his capital to Pataliputra from Vaisali, where Sisunaga had transferred the seat of his government from Rajgir, when he had come from Benares. Mahapadma Nanda is recorded in the Puranas as a second Parasurama, who, being very valiant and avaricious, extirpated the Kshatriyas and brought the whole earth under one umbrella. Adding an other rampart to the rising city, he built a palace of stone, whose carvings and ornaments were of extraordinary skill, and about which the Chinese pilgrims record a tradition that it was erected by the genii. He is said to be the Chandasoka, who constructed a large hell, known as "hell" or "earth-prison." Asokavadana, a Nepalese manuscript on the life of Asoka, records that Kalasoka [illegible], the son of a rich merchant, who was seized by his jailor, Chandagirika, converted the king to Buddhism. By the advice of another Jain priest, named Yasa, he erected chaityas at Rajagriha, Barnagrama and other places, and invited from Urumunda hill [illegible], near Mathura, Upagupta, the fourth Mahasthavira of the Buddhist church, who pointed out to him all the sacred spots, visited by the Buddha, for the erection of stupas and directed him to go on pilgrimage to Mahabodhi and Kapilavastu. This pilgrimage is most probably referred to in the Pali inscription of the pillar lately discovered at the Lumbini garden in the Nepal Terai. From the fact that Upagupta, who was initiated in 100 A.B. (443 B.C.), was the spiritual guide of Asoka, I infer that all the monuments, constructed with the help of the genii (Yakshas), might be ascribed to Kalasoka, and not to Dharmasoka, whose date was Mogaliputta, in about 230 A.B. (313 B.C.), and who most probably raised the "mountain" structures, referred to by Hiuen Tsiang. Thus did Mr. Smith of Gorakhpur, a great authority on antiquarian matters, observe in his illustrated pamphlet of 1896 on the "Remains near Kasia," that "that Emperor" (meaning Asoka) "has obtained credit for more buildings than any sovereign could possibly have erected."

Vitasoka, the brother of the king, being instigated by the Tirthikas, who were jealous of the Buddhists gaining royal patronage, raised a revolt to gain the throne. But he was afterwards defeated and imprisoned. Owing to the protection of Upagupta, he became a Buddhist monk under the guidance of the latter's disciple [illegible], and retired to [illegible] [illegible] for the purpose of [illegible] meditation. Having thus he had become a great saint, Kalasoka invited his younger brother to reside at the capital, where he built for him a monastery in imitation of the hill, as narrated by the Chinese pilgrims, who name him Mahendra by mistake.

In the 10th year of his reign, and 443 B.C., the Vajjiputtakas of Vaisali entered the Sangha. In whose time the second Buddhistic Council was held at Vaisali, now Basra, two years after 443 B.C.; and Kalasoka of Pataliputra was the last point to attend and complete the meeting of the 700 Theras. But the Vajjiputtakas, who were excommunicated by the council, gained another party, thus becoming [illegible] to 10,000, who, according to Asvaghosha, in his life of Buddha, held a great meeting, called the Mahasangiti, which [illegible] the [illegible] and other Sutras of their own. In this way five schools were formed—Mahasangiti, Dharmaguptika, Mahisasaka, Kasyapiya, and Sarvastivadins—each having its own peculiar and distinctive doctrines. In 137 A.B. (406 B.C.) King Nanda Mahapadma, being in great doubt as to which party was right, convened at Pataliputra all the Aryas to bring out the means to agree with the [illegible], and, according to the advice of some priests, allied with the [illegible], being the party of the Vajjians of Vaisali. But after, for 88 years, the [illegible] continued to [illegible] among themselves, the [illegible] alternately subdividing into eighteen. One hundred and two years later, the [illegible] [illegible] the [illegible].

Kalasoka reigned 28 years, and was succeeded by his [illegible] sons, of whom the eldest was Bhadrasena. They all reigned one after the other for 22 years. The last brother was [illegible], who had a Sudra concubine. She gave birth to [illegible], who, killing his father, usurped the throne of Pataliputra, under the title of Ugrasena-Nanda,* in 1[illegible] A.B. ([illegible] B.C.). He with his eight brothers, [illegible] known as the nine Nandas, reigned for a period of 22 years. They were the [illegible] of the Brahmanas, and gave them money and food in the palace. One of these Nandas was known as [illegible] (Nandaraja), who had, according to Puranic [illegible], an army of 20,000 horse, 2,000 foot, 2,000 chariots, and 3,000 elephants.

The name of the last Nanda was Dhana-Nanda, so called from his great riches, which [illegible] mentions a tradition that he [illegible] five treasures, [illegible] identified as the five lost Stupas erected with special magnificence by Asoka. [illegible] was his chief pandit. Among the Brahmanas, whom Dhana-Nanda used to feed daily in his palace, once appeared an extraordinary astrologer, who [illegible] to be [illegible]. He is well known as Chanakya, native of Chanaka, who was the author of a [illegible], and [illegible] probably [illegible] the [illegible]. Because the king got angry with him, who, not getting the chief place as [illegible] priest, [illegible], and crossing the threshold of the [illegible], [illegible] away in disgrace to Takshasila (Taxila) in Panjab. But to plot the destruction of the Nanda dynasty the more effectively, Chanakya returned to the [illegible] country, of which the [illegible] was most probably that now known as [illegible], and saw [illegible] military [illegible], named Chandragupta, with marks of royalty, at [illegible] now [illegible]. If I am right in my [illegible], and as [illegible] him for 1,000 silver pieces. Instructing him in the different [illegible] of [illegible], Chanakya, also known as Vishnugupta and [illegible], minutely explained to him the line of action for attaining royalty.—Bigandet's *Gaudama*, Volume II, Chapter V, pages 128 to 137.

The Jaina chronicles, as recorded in the *Parisishta*, say that Chanakya was the son of a devout Jaina Brahman of Chanaka, a village in the [illegible] (Chanagama ?). He went to Pataliputra to get [illegible] from Nanda, who, however, was very [illegible] with him for his [illegible]. [illegible] that he would destroy the king, Chanakya fled to the village of King's Peacocks, Mayura-poshaka (Mayura, near [illegible], in [illegible]), where he saw Chandragupta, the son of the chief's daughter. The boy used to be [illegible] in [illegible] as king by the children of the village, while [illegible] in the field. Promising him a kingdom, Chanakya brought him, and [illegible] troops with the money that he had acquired, laid siege to Pataliputra. But they were easily vanquished by the more numerous army of the Nanda; and Chanakya and Chandragupta were forced to run away, pursued by the enemy's horsemen. They escaped to Himavat-kuta (Nepal ?), and allying with Parvataka, the king of the country, [illegible] the campaign by reducing the [illegible] provinces. The allies at last captured the capital and expelled Dhana-Nanda, whose daughter, however, Chandragupta married and ascended the throne in 1[illegible] A.V. ([illegible] B.C.). The Buddhist chronicles, however, differ from the Jaina account by stating that Dhana-Nanda was killed, and that Chandragupta became king in 1[illegible] A.B. ([illegible] B.C.), a difference of eight years.† The destruction of the Nanda dynasty is narrated in an interesting Sanskrit drama, called *Mudra Rakshasa*, by Vishakadatta, the son of Prithu-Maharaja (see Wilson's translation).

MAURYA DYNASTY.

The Buddhistic chronicles relegate the origin of the Mauryas to a prehistoric period when they, being a collateral branch of the Sakyas of Kapilavastu, retired, according to the *Mahavamsa* [illegible], [illegible] mountains, and "discovered a delightful location, well watered and situated in the midst of [illegible] trees." There they founded a town, which was called by its Sakya lords "Moriya-nagara," or "Mayura-nagara," the town of Peacocks, presumably from the fact of an abundance of peacocks when the first settlers saw them. Asvaghosha, the 12th patriarch, in his [illegible] of the Buddha, calls the dynasty *Maurya*. The Jaina chronicles say that it was the village of the king's peacocks (Mayura-poshaka). But the Brahmanical Puranas derive the word Maurya from Mura, the [illegible] queen of Mahapadma-Nanda, the mother or grandmother of Chandragupta. This prehistoric town of Moriya-nagara I propose to identify with the site [illegible], and [illegible] to [illegible], now known as [illegible].

A portion of the Mauryas appears to have subsequently moved about six miles [illegible] and founded Pippalivana, literally the Forest of Pipal Trees (now [illegible]),

* [illegible]

† There appears to be a difference of eight years between the [illegible] of the [illegible] and the [illegible].

where king raised a stupa over the ashes of Gautama-Buddha they had received at Kusinagara (now [illegible]). A branch of the Pipphalivana Mauryas appears to have migrated again to Nepal, on the conquest of which by Ajatasatru in [illegible] B.C., they had to fly eastward, where they for the third time founded a town, calling it Mauryanagara after [illegible]. Further misfortune falling on them, they had again to fly precipitately. A princess of theirs was in the family way, who was brought to Pipphalivana. There she gave birth to a son, whom she cast away. The child was taken in and adopted by a [illegible], Chanakya by name, from whom he received the well-known appellation of Chandragupta, having been protected (gupta) by [illegible].*

On becoming the king of Magadha, Chandragupta appointed Chanakya, hitherto his guide and benefactor, as his prime minister. Parvataka, his ally, dying shortly after, the king took possession of his dominions in the Himalayas. As some of the last Nanda's followers continually committed daring robberies, and otherwise gave trouble to the establishment of the new government, Chanakya appointed a weaver, who succeeded in restoring order and in killing all robbers.

No events of his reign of 24 years were recorded, except that there was a great famine which lasted twelve years, which compelled the Jaina [illegible] to go to some other country, some of as Chandragupta [illegible], and favoured the Brahmans. Bhadrabahu, the head of the Jaina church (367-[illegible] B.C.)†, who is said to have converted the king, went to Nepal. The monks, who remained at Pataliputra, neglected their regular studies so that the sacred lore was in the point of falling into oblivion. The Jaina church, therefore, [illegible] at the capital, when the famine was over, collected the fragments which they could remember, and which are now known as the eleven Angas. Sthulabhadra, the son of [illegible], who was the prime minister to the ninth Nanda (Dhana-Nanda), was the disciple of Bhadrabahu, and after his death became the head of the church (357-[illegible] B.C.). In some Jaina legends, Chandragupta is said to have retired from the worldly life and died by [illegible] in about [illegible] B.C.

A great famine and the Jaina to Nepal.

[illegible] conversion to the Jaina [illegible].

Chanakya placed on the throne his son, Bindusara, who was born of Durdhara, the queen: he was then in his [illegible] year. Chanakya appears to have been subsequently overshadowed by a rival minister. The reign of Bindusara, who was also called [illegible], appears to be uneventful, he dying in 214 A.B. (329 B.C.), after ruling for [illegible] years. According to the Buddhists, both he and his father were the followers of the Brahmans.

Bindusara.

Bindusara left 101 sons, of whom Sumana or Susima was the eldest. His first queen, Dharma, gave birth to two sons, Asoka and Tissa. Asoka was sent in his [illegible] year as Governor of Ujjain, or, according to [illegible], to Taxasila, to quell a rebellion. Hearing of the danger and illness of his father, he came back to the capital at the age of [illegible] years after an absence of several years, and on his death, usurped the throne with the help of the chief minister, Radhagupta, through whose intrigue Susima had to [illegible] to Taxasila. On his return, Susima attacked Pataliputra; but Asoka defeated and slew him along with all his brothers. He then became the king, being crowned in 218 A.B. (325 B.C.), under the title of Priyadarsi. He was the 10th or, according to others the [illegible] successor from Ajatasatru.

On Susima's death, his wife fled in disguise to [illegible], a village a little east of Pataliputra, where she shortly after gave birth to a son, named Nigrodha. This boy entered the monastic order under Varuna, whose monastery was a little distant from the southern gate of the capital. While one morning Nigrodha was going towards the eastern gate to visit his mother at [illegible], Asoka, who was then strolling on the king's gate enjoying the cool morning air, saw and called him, and conversing with him on matters of faith, was converted by him in the fourth year after his coronation. Subsequently Tissa Moggaliputra, the sixth patriarch, 319—[illegible] B.C., became his spiritual teacher.

Asoka Priyadarsi.

In order to acquire religious merit, Asoka built a great number of stupas in all the cities of Jambudwipa, distributing the Buddha's relics, which he extracted from the stupas, previously raised at Vaisali, Kapilavastu, Allakappa, [illegible], Ramagrama, and Rajgriha. At Rajgriha, the king found the greatest quantity of relics, which [illegible] had collected and buried in an underground structure in about [illegible] A.B. The finding out of the relics happened in [illegible] A.B., as [illegible] by the first [illegible] in an inscription on a golden plate. Having a [illegible] of the Buddha, the king gave orders for the multiplication of his statues and [illegible] their [illegible]. In [illegible] he issued a proclamation inviting the people to observe the eight precepts of the Buddhistic doctrines. He gave orders for the erection of the stupas in [illegible] A.B., which were completed and dedicated three years afterwards. The first stupa that he built was at his capital at Pataliputra, which the Chinese pilgrims described as very magnificent.

For the 84,000 monasteries.

To propagate the new state religion with better effect, [illegible] in Magadha, Asoka commissioned his own son and daughter, Mahendra and Sanghamitra, in [illegible] A.B. And

* [illegible]

† [illegible]

to expel the heretics from the church, and to reconcile all sectarian differences, he invited Tissa, then seventy-two years old, from Ahoganga (near Hardwar?), to hold the third Buddhistic Council in 235 A.B. (= [illegible] B.C.), when the genuineness of the canon of the scriptures, as recorded by Kasyapa in the first council at Rajagriha, was confirmed and the purity of the doctrine restored. The assembly was held at Kukkutarama, where a vast hall was erected, at the end of which a fine pavilion made of cloth of various and bright colours was prepared for the accommodation of the monarch. Each Bhikshu was here examined, and those found wanting in the knowledge and practice of the three Pitakas were expelled from the assembly, being stripped of the monastic robe and were made to wear the white dress of the householder ([illegible]). After the termination of the third council, missionaries were sent to different countries to preach Buddhism, and Asoka deputed Mahendra and Sanghamitra with a branch of the Bodhi tree at Buddha-Gaya to Ceylon, where Tissa was reigning at the time.

3rd Buddhistic Council and purification of Buddhism.

[illegible] missionaries abroad and Buddhism in Ceylon.

Being in terms of amity with Dharmasoka, Tissa had despatched a costly present of gems and pearls to Pataliputra, and the monarch of Jambudwipa, not to be outdone in generosity, [illegible] the Ceylonese embassy, and sent them back with his own [illegible] and ambassadors bearing gifts of a chamara, a sword of state, a royal parasol, golden slippers, a head ornament, a vase of gold, Ganges water, [illegible] and a great number of minor articles. As advised by Asoka, Tissa with his subjects embraced the Buddhistic religion and otherwise followed the instructions of the royal envoys. [illegible], the queen and other ladies became nuns [illegible] under his sister.

From a line of arguments, embodied in a separate note, I conclude that Asoka was the Greek Sandrokottos or Sandrakyptos, the contemporary of Seleukos Nikator. While at Takshasila (Taxila) where Bindusara sent him to quell a rebellion, he appears to have visited and offended Alexander the Great in his camp. Justin records that when he offended the Greek invader by his impertinent language, who ordered him to be put to death. But young Sandrokottos escaped by flight. Fatigued with long journey, he laid down to rest, when a lion of large size is said to have come and licked off the perspiration without harming him. This prodigy inspired him, and collecting a band of robbers and rousing the Indians, he waged war with the captains of Alexander. In the battles he fought with the Greeks, he was always distinguished in the van, being mounted on an elephant of great size and strength. Seleukos Nikator, being defeated at last in about 300 B.C., entered into a treaty with the Maurya emperor, to whom he gave his daughter, ceded considerable territories west of Indus, and sent Megasthenes as his ambassador. Megasthenes, who was in the camp of Sandrokottos which consisted of 400,000 men, did not witness on any day thefts exceeding the sum of 200 drachmas, and he noticed the rarity of crimes in India. The king, who, besides his family name, adopted, like his predecessors, the surname of Palibothra, conquered the whole of India, with 600,000 men and 9,000 elephants, of which he gave 500 to Seleukos.

[illegible]

Megasthenes wrote an account of what he saw in India, and describes Palibothra (Pataliputra) as 80 stadia in length and 15 in breadth. "It is of the shape of a parallelogram, and is girded with wooden walls pierced with loopholes for the discharge of arrows. It has a ditch in front for defence and for receiving the sewage of the city." The ditch was 600 cubits in breadth and 30 in depth. "The wall was crowned with 570 towers and had four and sixty gates." "The greatest city in India" in the dominion of the Prasians (Prachyas), who were the most distinguished in all India, was where the Ganges, whose breadth was 100 stadia, and depth 20 fathoms at least, and Erannoboas (Hiranyavaha, the gold-bearing, so-called from the yellow sands of the Sone) united. Megasthenes adds further on that the city extended in the inhabited quarters to an extreme length on each side of 80 stadia with a breadth of 15. "Such cities as are situated on the banks of rivers or on the sea coast were built of wood, being meant to last only for a time; so destructive are the heavy rains, which pour down, and the rivers also, when they overflow their banks and inundate the plains; while those cities which stand on commanding situations and lofty eminences are built of brick and mud." This remark applies to Pataliputra; for the suburb, south of the capital, which was, as now, flooded annually, possessed wooden structures, as my excavations showed; while the metropolis itself contained brick and stone buildings.

Asoka had a eventful reign of 37 years. His edicts on rocks and pillars are too well known to be detailed here. One of his sons, by name Kustana, founded the Khotan kingdom in 234 A.B. (= [illegible] B.C.). Kunala, the heir-apparent, was sent to Taxila to quell a rebellion, most probably raised in connection with the establishment of the Greek kingdom in Bactria; there he was blinded at the instigation of one of the queens, who wanted to secure the throne for her own son, who was then governor of Ujjayini.

[illegible]

In 248 A.B. (= [illegible] B.C.), Queen Asandhimitra died; and three years after Asoka married a second queen, who tried to destroy the Bodhi tree at Bodha Gaya; and she probably it was who caused Kunala to be blinded at Takshasila. Thus mortified and otherwise fatigued with royal and worldly life, Asoka retired and became an ascetic in 254 A.B., and died two years after in great poverty; for he could not present to the temple more than a half apple, as referred to by Hiuen Tsiang.

Samprati, the grandson and son of Kunala, ascended the throne of Pataliputra in 234 A.B. (=269 B.C.), or, according to the Jaina chronicles, in 230 A.V. (=2[illegible] B.C.)—a difference of only three years.

[illegible]

A legend is recorded in the Buddhistic chronicles of Nepal, that before he died, Asoka ordered his grandson to present the whole kingdom to the Buddhistic church, which Samprati, by the advice of Radhagupta, his minister, bought back for four crores of gold pieces. According to the Parisishta, he became a staunch Jaina under Suhastin, the 11th Sthavira (from 246 to 292 B.C.), whom he met at Ujjayini. Samprati was the 17th successor from Srenika Bimbisara. He erected Jaina monuments in his extensive empire, adorning the Jinalayas with Pratimas, and other edifices, and erected a [illegible] in Anarya (foreign) country. The advice and example of Samprati induced his vassals to embrace the Jaina creed, and caused Jaina temples to be erected over the whole of Jambudvipa and the adjacent countries, whereas also to the Andhras and the Dravidas missionaries were sent. He died at the end of his reign, and the Jainas thus losing their royal patron, rapidly lost their ascendancy at Pataliputra, and, soon after the death of Sthulabhadra, the son of the minister of the 9th Nanda, and the 8th head of the Jaina church in 208 B.C., his two disciples, Mahagiri and Suhastin, separated from each other. The latter, the spiritual guide of the late king, had therefore to remove to Ujjayini, which henceforth appears to have become the head-quarters of the Jaina church.

Samprati appears to have been referred to by Athenaios as Amitrochates or Allitrochades (Amitra-ghata), the son of Sandrocottus, who once wrote to Antiochus asking him to buy and send him sweet wine, dried figs, and a sophist. Antiochus replied—"We shall send you the figs and the wine; but in Greece custom forbids a sophist to be sold." To Allitrochades at Pataliputra Daimachos was sent on an embassy by Antiochus, who had before deputed Megasthenes to Sandrocottus.

According to "The Questions of Manjusri," the grandson of the Maurya Asoka (Asoka), by name Pushyamitra (Samprati), succeeding to the empire, persecuted the Buddhists, destroying the pagodas and the scriptures. Five hundred Arhats, however, escaped. A righteous king succeeding, 500 priests recovered the law from the [illegible], and again taught the people. The king divided the Dharma Vinaya into parts and built a stupa to preserve them, so that it became difficult for the people to consult them. An old Sthavira (monk) wrote a commentary, selecting such passages from the Vinaya of the "Great congregation," as in accordance with the Kasyapiya school. The other party, however, included false additions. The king at last decided at Pataliputra between the two schools by the method of slips of wood, black and white. Those Bhikshus taking the black slips were in far greater number than those who chose the white. Thus the Buddhistic church (Sangha) separated into the old Mahasanghikas and the new Sthaviras.

Persecution of the Buddhists.

Afterwards there was a wicked king in Pataliputra, from whom all the Sramanas fled, and the sacred books were scattered far and wide. A good king succeeding to the throne, the Buddhists were again invited to Pataliputra. At this time 500 priests wanted to decide matters of faith, but there was no copy of the Vinaya to refer to, or a teacher who knew it. They then sent a priest to Jetavana at Sravasti, to copy out the Vinaya in the original character, as it had been handed down to that time. Fa Hian long after copied out this Sanskrit original, in 417 A.D., at the Asrama of Asoka, or the Vihara of the southern Devaraja (Virudhaka).

Re-establishment of the Buddhism.

Pataliputra had become the head quarters of the Buddhist church from the time when it became the capital city; and the Sthaviras from Upagupta, who was initiated in [illegible] A.B. downwards, used to reside here. The 10th, 11th and the 12th Sthaviras—Parsva, Mahatyaga and Asvaghosha—are especially mentioned in the Buddhistic literature as residents of this city. Asvaghosha, a great poet and singer who was born at Benares, used to travel about with a body of musicians and to convert many persons of distinction. In this way he converted 500 young princes of Pataliputra by publicly chanting hymns, which practice on that account was prohibited by the king. Itsing says that the hymns used in the Buddhistic church, when he visited India in about 675 A.D., were composed by Asvaghosha, who also wrote the well-known life of the Buddha, that was translated into Chinese in 420 A.D. Hiuen Tsiang mentions that Asvaghosha defeated a learned Brahman near Kusumapura who had for a long time silenced all Buddhist speakers. The King of [illegible] invaded Magadha and besieged the capital; and at the intercession of Asvaghosha went back, with some relics. This invasion is most probably that led by Kanishka, who took away the Sthavira himself to Gandhara.

After the departure of Asvaghosha, and when the generation of learned Buddhists passed away, Hiuen Tsiang records that the heretic teachers of the [illegible] gave themselves up to study of the scriptures with a view to gain mastery; and summoning their partisans in their homes, struck the ghanta (bell), and addressing the king to be the umpire, challenged the orthodox Buddhists to discuss with them. The latter, though numerous, were weak and not so learned as their enemy, and hence were easily defeated. From that time they were bound not to strike the bell in any monastery. After twelve years Aryadeva, the great disciple of Nagarjuna and the 15th Sthavira, secretly entering the city and loudly striking the ghanta, challenged and defeated the heretics in the presence of the king, who erected the Bell monument to commemorate this event.

Returning to political history, we enter a dark period, for no mention of any successor to Samprati is found in the chronicles of either the Jainas or of the Brahmans.* The *Puranas* alone give the names and duration of the different dynasties. According to some, the Maurya dynasty consisted of ten kings who altogether reigned 137 years, and after Asoka, Suyasa (Samprati), [illegible], [illegible], Somasarma, Satadhanva and Vrihadratha successively sat on the throne of Pataliputra. The last Maurya king was dethroned and killed by his minister, Pushpamitra, who established the Sunga dynasty in about 180 B.C. The Sunga kings were ten in number, who reigned for 112 years. This dynasty was succeeded by that of the Kanva, which had five kings reigning for 45 years. After them came the Andhras from Deccan, whose duration was 456 years.

* [illegible] "The Chronicles of King Kharavela" [illegible] [illegible] [illegible] the king [illegible] [illegible] [illegible].

Sunga, Kanva and Andhra.

But it is very doubtful that the Andhras had an undisputed possession of Magadha for such a length of time. Major Wilford states that the Andhras lived at [illegible] and [illegible], some miles south-west of Pataliputra. Taranath, the Tibetan historian, mentions a great number of Magadha kings, who, however, are so unchronologically treated, that it is very difficult to adjust them in their proper places. The Tibetan records that during the usurpation of Pushpamitra, the Tirthikas invaded India and destroyed temples from Jalandhara to Magadha, and the usurper had to fly and to die five years after.* Taranath mentions another invasion of Magadha by Hunimanta, the king of the white Huns of Persia, who also [illegible] temples during the reign of [illegible] Chandra. Buddhapaksha, his latter's contemporary, [illegible] king of Benares, allied with Chinese, and with the aid of the kings of Western and Central India defeated and slew the invader, and re-established Buddhism.

Invasion of Magadha by the Tartars.

Notwithstanding these invasions, Pataliputra continued to be a capital city. The king of Persia (China) sent an ambassador to the Maharaja [illegible] of Magadha, between 350 and 378 A.D. This Chinese officer records that "the palaces of the fortified city, in which he" (the king) "resided, were watered by canals, which formed on all sides and filled the deep ditches, which surrounded the city. Beneath it flowed a great river" (Ganges). "All the palaces and public buildings of the city were covered with inscriptions and other ornaments in relief. A winding street, one li in length, formed the market. The houses were several storeys in height." This probably refers to the present Chauk of Patna, north of which was the citadel.

Pataliputra still the capital.

Towards the close of the third century A.D., Pandu was the emperor reigning at Pataliputra. He was at first of Brahmanical persuasion. Guhasiva was the king of Kalinga, subordinate to him, who was a devout Buddhist and worshipped a stupa at Dantapura, his capital. The left tooth of the Buddha, which had been brought by Khema Thera from Kusinagara, was enshrined in this stupa. Pandu asked this celebrated relic from Guhasiva, who, however, declined to part with it. Thereupon Pandu's Chittayana, at the command of the emperor, besieged Dantapura and brought the relic and Guhasiva as prisoner to Pataliputra. Seeing the miracles wrought by the tooth, Pandu became a Buddhist and built a splendid temple over it. Kshiradhara, king of Sravasti, besieged Pataliputra to possess the tooth, but was defeated and slain. The relic was subsequently taken back to Dantapura and thence to Ceylon for safe custody.

Pandu.

The next fragmentary notice that is found in connection with the history of Pataliputra is of the Gupta dynasty, which was most probably established here by Chandragupta I in 319 A.D. If Alberuni's statement be true that the date of the extinction of the Gupta dynasty coincides with the commencement of the Balabhi dynasty. The *Vishnu Purana* records that the Guptas reigned in Magadha. According to Mr. Fleet, Chandra Gupta I married a princess of the Lichchhavi family of Pataliputra, which presumably came from Vaisali. Mr. Smith of [illegible] states in his "Observations on the Gupta Coinage," that "I have no doubt that Pataliputra was ordinarily the capital of Chandra Gupta I, Samudra Gupta, and of Chandra Gupta II in his earlier years. But after the annexation of Surashtra (Guzerat) and the intervening countries, Pataliputra lay inconveniently far to the east, and there are some reasons for thinking that Ayodhya became at least the headquarters of the Gupta empire.... It is possible that Pataliputra may have continued to be one of the royal residences in the time of Chandra Gupta's successors, but I do not think it probable that the centre of their power lay in that city." In the history of China, King Kieto [illegible] or Gupta, whose family was reigning for several generations, is related as sending an embassy to China in 405 A.D. In my excavations here, I found two Gupta coins, belonging to Chandragupta II, and since these two were the last ones of the number of old coins I found here, it seems reasonable to conclude that Pataliputra ceased to be a capital city about this time, even as Mr. Smith suggests.

Gupta.

The next fragmentary notice of Pataliputra is by Fa Hian (Fa Hsian), according to S. Beal, who visited it in about 415 A.D. He saw in the middle of the city the royal palace and halls which Asoka (? Kalasoka) was believed to have commissioned the Asuras to construct by piling

Fa Hian's visit.

---

* This is [illegible] referred to in the *Vayu Purana* of the [illegible] [illegible] [illegible] that —

* That the [illegible] Tirthikas, after [illegible] Pushpamitra [illegible] [illegible] of [illegible] [illegible] Pataliputra, [illegible] [illegible] [illegible] [illegible]. The [illegible] [illegible] [illegible] to [illegible]. There will be a [illegible] [illegible] [illegible] kingdom [illegible] [illegible] to [illegible] [illegible].

* [illegible] of the temples [illegible] [illegible] [illegible] [illegible] from the banks of the Jumna to [illegible], Bihar and Magadha. — [illegible].

up streets, and of which the walls and gates showed elegant carving and inlaid sculpture—work of a style no human hand could accomplish. About the site of the [illegible], the Chinese pilgrim notes that every year, on the 8th of the 2nd Chinese month, there was held the festival of the procession of about twenty cars, every one of which was differently decorated. A car was a wooden tower, four-storied and pagoda-like, which was about 22 feet in height and had five stages with corner shrines (cupolas?). It was made of bamboos lashed together, the whole structure being supported by a centre-post resembling a large spear with three points. In each of these was a figure of a Buddha with a Bodhisattva in attendance, along with the statues of the Brahmanical devas,—all adorned with gold, silver and glass and under canopies of embroidered silk,—was carried in procession.* At this time the Brahmacharis used to invite the Buddhas to enter the city, where they stayed for a night or two, burning lamps and making religious offerings amidst music and games. From the fact of the invitation by the Brahmans, it appears that the Buddhists did not at this time live within the city, but outside it, chiefly at the two convents, Mahayana and Hinayana, near the great stupa of Asoka, where about 700 priests dwelt. There were two celebrated Brahman teachers, of whom one was much respected by the king. Fa Hian resided here for more than three years, in the [illegible] (Vihara), learning and copying Buddhist scriptures, which he could not get elsewhere.

Fa Hian also records that of all the kingdoms of mid-India, Madhyadesa, the towns of Magadha were especially large. The people were rich and prosperous, practising virtue and justice. The nobles and householders founded hospitals and dispensaries within the city, to which the poor and the destitute, crippled and the diseased, repaired for lodging and medical treatment. "Physicians," he says, "inspect their diseases, and according to their cases order them food and drink, medicines and decoctions—everything, in fact, that may contribute to their ease. When cured, they depart at their convenience."—Beal's "Records of the Western World," volume I, Introduction.

After the departure of Fa Hian, the site appears to have been deserted by the kings, who, with the court, removed elsewhere. Pataliputra then rapidly declined; for after a prosperity of over three [illegible] years, as foretold by the Buddha, the fate of Pataliputra was decreed by fire, inundation and internal dissensions. Of the last cause of destruction we have no historical or traditional record, but we can form an idea from the civil wars of the Nanda and Maurya dynasties, as described in the *Mudra Rakshasa* (*Minister's Seal*), translated by Professor Wilson in his *Hindu Theatre*. As to fire, we have ample evidence even now, for the city, even as now, was composed of wooden and tiled houses which are easily affected by fire during the hot season. The flood also appears during the rainy season; and the ancient city must have been submerged at exceptionally wet periods. This fact explains the formation of a yellowish and reddish silt, from 6 to 12 feet in depth, above the débris of ancient times.

Pataliputra ceases to be the capital and begins to decay.

The royal patronage being gone and the city being thus deserted, the Buddhist establishments had to starve or to depart from here. Many went to Nalanda, which became a great university of Buddhistic learning. In [illegible] A.D. Arhat Kasyapa of the Maurya family left the convent of the Pandit [illegible] and went to Tibet (Bod-Yul), where seven years after he built the first monastery, near the great site of the country. Rockhill, in his "Life of the Buddha" from the Tibetan sources, notes that five monks from Magadha visited the then reigning king, Lha-tho-tho-ri, at [illegible], and presented and explained to him some relics.

[illegible] deserted by the Buddhists [illegible]

Pataliputra decayed so rapidly after this period that, when Hiuen Tsiang visited it in 637 A.D., all the monasteries that he describes were in complete ruins, so that he could not have passed more than seven days in the "Little City." He, however, gives a somewhat detailed account of the Buddhist monuments that he saw. Magadha at this time was [illegible]. The walled towns had but few inhabitants. The country being low was inundated during the rains. "From the first month of summer to the second month of autumn. The villages, which were thickly populated, were raised on elevated spots, and communication was kept up by boats, [illegible]. Rice of an unusual kind was grown here; known as the rice of the great."

Hiuen Tsiang's description of the city in 637 A.D.

The old city of Pataliputra was 70 li round and was long deserted,—of which the foundation walls only existed; and on the river bank and to the north of the old palace there was a small town consisting of about one thousand houses. At that time there were one hundred Sangharamas of which fifty and one hundred temples were hardly traceable out of which only two or three existed entire at the time of Hiuen Tsiang, who, however, adds that these monasteries, Deva temples and stupas which lie in ruins may be counted by hundreds.†

This lamentable state of decay was aggravated by Sasanka, king of Karnasuvarna, who, some years before the arrival of Hiuen Tsiang, invaded Magadha and destroyed the Buddhist monuments. And at Pataliputra, or rather near the small town of [illegible], he attempted to break into pieces the sacred stone of the Buddha's footprints on which traces, and the great relic

Invasion by Sasanka who destroys the Buddhist monuments.

* [illegible] translation of Fa Hian [illegible]

† [illegible] Hiuen Tsiang [illegible]

‡ [illegible] party.

had stood for the last time. But Pūrṇavarma, the last of the Aśoka's race, and subordinate to Śāśāṅka of Karṇa[illegible], was defeated and expelled the invaders, restored or rebuilt some of the sacred edifices.

After the departure of Hiuen Tsiang, no mention of Pāṭaliputra is found in any records. I-tsing, the third Chinese pilgrim, who visited Magadha in about 670 A.D., did not visit it; nor the first Muhammadan invasion under Bakhtiyar Khilji in 1199 appear to touch it. In 1[illegible], however, the inhabitants of Patna [illegible], then a part of Bihar, are mentioned in one of the early Muhammadan history, as [illegible] with [illegible] and stopping all intercourse between Delhi and Bengal. Patna strongly [illegible], and a fort was ordered to be constructed here. This is probably the present [illegible] of Patna at the east end of the city. In [illegible] the Pathan sardar of Bihar [illegible] at Patna and [illegible] Sher Khan of his government, and named Muhammad, [illegible] of [illegible], as king of Bihar.

Sher Shah rebuilds Patna in 1541.

In 1541, Sher Shah, [illegible] the empire, built a citadel here on the sites of the ancient town. The inscription, dated 1042 H., on the gate of the fort, however, attributes its erection to [illegible] Khan. Shah Amir, a native of the Panjab, settled here in the [illegible], now known as Dargah, as his name was [illegible] in 1062 H. In [illegible] A.D., Khurram, the son of Jahangir, seized Patna, the then capital of Bihar, and taking possession of the palace, women and wealth of the Subah gave his troops to plunder. Shah Jahan, when in rebellion resided at the palace of the [illegible] at Patna. Azim, the grandson of Aurangzeb, was afterwards the Subah of Bihar and repaired the old fortification, whence the town got the name of Azimabad.

Pandit Haraprasad Sastri, in his last year's pamphlet on "Living Buddhism in Bengal," notices in the Library of the Asiatic Society, Calcutta, a manuscript called *[illegible]*, which gives an account of Pāṭaliputra or Patna town, by Jagannātha[illegible], a learned scholar and a great traveller, at the command of Vaijala Bengali, the [illegible] proprietor of the pargana about the city of Patna. Vaijala died in 1[illegible] A.D., [illegible] but the [illegible] was [illegible] shortly after. Jagannātha mentions another Raja, [illegible], a Buddhist, who conquered Patna and other towns.

In [illegible] *[illegible]*, a Jaina work, it is prophesied that 1,914 years after the death of Vira in 1419 A.D., Kalkin, after committing many disasters and destroying the temples at Mathura, will become king. An inundation of 17 days will occupy him and his subjects who [illegible] to Pāṭaliputra, where, digging the ground, [illegible] Nanda, and [illegible] his treasures, will rebuild the town. After persecuting the Jainas, Kalkin will die in 2000 A.V. or 1[illegible] A.D. This might refer to the rebuilding of the town by Sher Shah, who, being a Muhammadan and Pathan, must have destroyed and ignored the ancient monuments while constructing the fort.

CHAPTER II. SECTION I. PRESENT STATE OF THE RUINS OF PĀṬALIPUTRA.*

Boundary of the ancient city.

Pāṭaliputra may reasonably be said to have included the long and narrow tract of the country from the suburbs of Bankipur village to Jafar Khan's garden, east of Patna, an extent of nearly nine miles or 80 stadia of Megasthenes. But the tradition, according to Martin's *Eastern India*, volume I, that the ancient Government or boundary extended from Bhagpur to Bana[illegible]. On the west of the village of Bankipur is a large expanse of low fields, which is annually flooded, and is still known as *Mar Son*, the dead Son, whose current is seen in rains flowing to the Ganges during the rains. This was undoubtedly the confluence of the Ganges and Erannoboas (Hiranyavaha, the golden-flowing, the Sona, so called from the large and yellow sands that are [illegible]), which Megasthenes takes it in his description of Palibothra. Megasthenes also mentions the Sonos as a separate river from the Erannoboas, which appears to be a mistake, for, in Sanskrit, Sona and Hiranyavaha are synonymous terms applied by the Brahmanical writers to one river only.

Ancient bed of the Son.

A branch of the Son, whose main current was on the west of the village of Bankipur, appears to have been diverted towards the east, and [illegible] south of the ancient city, to form the ditch, which, according to the Greek account, was 600 feet in width. From the indications of low ground, 30 to 40 feet below the fields and [illegible], its course is easily traced on the south of the Bankipur station and railway line, Lohanipur, Bahadurpur, Rampur, on the north of which is the large tank of [illegible], and the [illegible]. From this tank the low fields [illegible] east[illegible] of the [illegible], and [illegible] Mahal [illegible] south of Patna, beyond which I have not yet followed it. About 10 feet below the [illegible] and reddish soil of the low fields is found a thick stratum of the large and thick yellowish sand peculiar to the Son, which the remains of ancient boats are occasionally discovered, as on the south of the present [illegible] and at [illegible], while digging tanks and wells. I also discovered a series of ancient [illegible], extending [illegible] feet in length and facing the south, in the north of Nayatola. This channel, which was turned into the ditch, 600 feet wide, thus ran parallel to the Ganges, and from the intervening strip thus formed and about a mile in width, which perceptibly slopes from the high river bank towards the south, we can easily understand the size of the ancient city as a parallelogram which Megasthenes describes in his *Indica*.

About half a mile south of the channel and the ditch of the city is a large expanse of low and marshy fields, where also large and yellowish sand, as also gravel [illegible], are seen. In

* See Plate I for a map of the city.

prehistoric time this was most probably the main channel of the Son, which joined with the [illegible], once about six miles further south, flowed here, and joined the Ganges at Patna, where a mosque with [illegible] religious building [illegible] is still [illegible] by the pilgrims [illegible], as also the villagers from distant places. This low tract is inundated during the rainy season, and the villages that are [illegible] here on elevated mounds, at long distances from one another, have communications only by boats, just as Hiuen Tsiang saw in the seventh century.

In the course of two thousand years and more, the silt from the Son and Ganges has accumulated over the ancient remains on the south of the city, to a height of about ten or twelve feet. And within the city itself, the débris of subsequent habitations has raised the present level of the ground to ten or fifteen feet. That a large amount of silt is brought in by the annual inundations of the Punpun and Son from the south and the west will be evident to one who sees the condition of the tract here during the rains. During the last rainy season, the whole suburb from Lohanipur to Bahadurpur, and [illegible] the south of the railway, was one sheet of running water supplied by streams from the south. And one day, viewing the country from the top of the gate at the village of [illegible], I saw in the north the Ganges, a [illegible]; in the west the wide expanse of the Son joining the former just [illegible] in a great current; and on the south, the whole looked like a [illegible] sea from the railway station far away to the south and south-east, the villages amidst palm trees looking as seen at long distances from one another; while the glorious scene of the suburbs, covering [illegible] garden [illegible] and [illegible], [illegible] towards the eastern horizon, where the [illegible] were washed up, and carried away in [illegible]. Only the long strip of the town, [illegible], [illegible] on the [illegible] waters that invaded it on all sides. The annual accumulation of silt can therefore be easily understood. Besides, the great amount of dust blown over here during the westerly winds must have added to the raising of the land. The people believe that such a yearly raised about the thickness of one wheat grain. The ruins of Pataliputra, therefore, lie deep under the earth; and, in order to trace out ancient monuments, I had to dig 20 feet and more in some places, as at Lohanipur and Kumrahar, to uncover the wooden palisade.

About two furlongs west of the Bankipore station is a mound, known as [illegible], which remains a [illegible] of ruins. From this place eastward, brick ruins are discovered here and there. About a mile south of the station is another mound near the village of Nawabganj, where I [illegible]; and less than a mile east of the latter is the village of Lohanipur, near which, and on the site of a traditional [illegible], my excavations proved very fruitful. About half-a-mile east of Lohanipur are two small villages, [illegible] and [illegible], which stand on two mounds, being about a furlong of each other. [illegible] appears to be an ancient mound in the midst of the bed of the Son and the city ditch. About half a mile north-east of Lohanipur [illegible] is the large mound known as [illegible], the hill of the [illegible], which Dr. Waddell identifies as the hermitage of Mahendra. Another [illegible] a mile east of [illegible] is the Dargah Arzani, which stands on an extensive mound. About two furlongs east of the Dargah is a large [illegible] mound of earth now utilised as a Muhammadan graveyard. And south of the Dargah and beyond the [illegible] is a number of ancient remains under the fields of [illegible], and in the elevated garden of [illegible], south of which and of the railway line I excavated a series of ghats or flights of brick steps that once fronted the Son on the north.

A furlong or so east, and a little south of the Son ghats, are extensive ruins at Kumrahar and the neighbouring villages. About half a mile south-east of Kumrahar is the large village of the two Paharis, Bar and Chhoti, large and small, which extending from north to south, for about three furlongs, show a large extent of mounds and high ground. About two furlongs north of the Chhoti Pahari, and just south of the railway line, is a very large and ancient well, which from its so-called unfathomable depth is called Agam Kuan. About a furlong east of Agam Kuan is a high mound, in the midst of an ancient tank, [illegible], [illegible] Jaina temples which enshrine [illegible] of the Tirthankaras, now occasionally worshipped by the followers of Mahavira.

About half a mile east of the [illegible] is the rectangular town of Patna, of which the ditch is clearly traceable on the west, south and the east, the north being washed by the Ganges. On the east and west of the town are two gates [illegible] Darwaza, [illegible] and [illegible], which presumably stand on ancient sites. In the [illegible], [illegible] traditional [illegible], are [illegible] of the pre-Muhammadan period. [illegible] east of the Patna railway station is a [illegible] and on the [illegible] on the bank of the Ganges is another, now connected with the grave of a Muhammadan saint. To the east and south of Patna, I have not yet been able to examine the country. Local tradition says that there were [illegible] (five) [illegible], [illegible] mounds, that were on the outskirts of the town. In the excavation of Mangal Talao in 1875, some walls and a wooden structure were found about 12 feet below the present level of the ground; and at [illegible], in a Muhammadan house, I have heard of a column pillar of the Asoka style.

As to the remains of the ancient palisade, I have traced it at Lohanipur, Bahadurpur, [illegible], [illegible], and south of Kumrahar. These wooden remains are generally 20 feet below the present level of the ground.

The vestiges of brick edifices were traced between 10 and 20 feet below ground. The double rampart or wall at Kumrahar went down to about 25 feet; while the comparatively modern buildings were exposed below 5 feet. But the more ancient structures—that of the Maurya period—were generally found between 8 and 18 feet. The bricks of the more ancient period were better burnt and grained, larger in size and more [illegible] in [illegible].

The traces of ancient [illegible] have been traced in all places. The fragments of stone [illegible], now worshipped as [illegible], are found everywhere. The two colossal statues of the Yakshas, taken to Calcutta at the end of the last century, were found probably in the [illegible] of [illegible], where I have discovered a large Asoka pillar and very interesting specimens of a carved Buddhistic railing. At [illegible] they are brought to light another Asoka pillar and a Buddhistic rail of a [illegible]. At the [illegible] were found several stone relics of Buddhistic rail posts and statues built into the walls of the local buildings; and here a finely-carved pillar on the [illegible] of the [illegible] shows [illegible]. A few winged lions were also found. Attached to a [illegible] of a modern temple at [illegible] are two carved jambs of an ancient [illegible]. In the neighbourhood of the temple of [illegible] and near a small tank were obtained several [illegible] of ancient art, one of which is now worshipped as the [illegible]. In the temple of the [illegible], are a fine statue of two [illegible], a [illegible] Mahadeva Lingam, and fragments of [illegible]. And near the [illegible] are [illegible] and a [illegible] figure of the Buddha. At [illegible], [illegible] and [illegible] are [illegible] of the past, both Buddhistic and Brahmanical. The [illegible] figure at [illegible] is most interesting, the [illegible] of the Maurya period [illegible]. It is [illegible], [illegible] being represented in the style of [illegible] at the time of the birth of Bodhisattva.

My excavations have yielded ancient coins, beads, and implements of iron. The coins range from the Punch marked to those of the Guptas. Several [illegible], peculiar to [illegible], were found. The beads are of different kinds, made in glass and crystal. The [illegible] of ancient pottery show graceful forms [illegible] by the [illegible] of to-day. The [illegible] of iron-ware consist of nails, spears, axes, &c., which possess the stamp of the ancient age.

CHAPTER II.—SECTION I.—[illegible] OF THE DIFFERENT [illegible] OF PATALIPUTRA*.

On a perusal of the foregoing history of Pataliputra, we find six periods of the great city. The first was prehistoric, being founded by [illegible] or his father, most probably on the site of the present Patna. The second was Pataligrama, most probably on the site of Patna, where Buddha preached and left his footprint. The third was the Nagara, constructed by Ajatasatru, of which the [illegible] gate was called after [illegible]. [illegible] appears to have completed it. The fourth was the capital of [illegible], who added [illegible], of which the circuit was [illegible]. The fifth was Palibothra, the city of Sandrocottus, described by Megasthenes as 80 stadia in length and 15 in breadth. The sixth is Patna of the Muhammadan period, and I may add that the seventh is [illegible] Patna of the English epoch, which we see growing in our midst. In two thousand and two hundred years the level of the country has been raised to twenty feet and more; and it will not be difficult to trace the [illegible] of the past where the soil has not yet been disturbed.

Seven periods of the city.

The Nagara of Ajatasatru must have been built of wood in the [illegible] style, as is evident from the rapidity of construction; for three years after, he invaded and conquered the Vaisali kingdom or [illegible] from this town, which served as the base of the military operations. The Chaitya of Pataligrama, in which the Buddha lodged and preached [illegible] to a [illegible], appears, however, to be an ordinary cabin as we see now in outlying villages, being [illegible] with thatch or tiles and having walls of mud. Kalasoka, about one hundred years after, on removing here, constructed an [illegible] rampart in order to extend the town to a larger area for the requirements of a capital.

Ajatasatru's and [illegible].

When the Maurya kingdom expanded into the Indian empire, Sandrocottus must have extended the capital still along the [illegible] of high land between the Ganges and the [illegible]. And here Megasthenes's account holds good; for he says that the rectangular city was 80 stadia (9⅕ miles) in length and 15 (1¾ miles) in breadth. Since there were sixty-four gates, the intervening space between two of them was about [illegible] feet [illegible]. From this calculation it appears that there were on each of the eastern and western walls five gates, of which the central one must have been the main [illegible] gate ([illegible]); while on north and the south and respectively [illegible] of which [illegible] probably were [illegible] gates. The northern gates led to the river [illegible]. As to the 570 towers with which the ancient palisade were defended and crowned, I think each of the gates had two bastions in front and two on the inner and [illegible] walls. Thus at the rate of four towers to a gate, we arrive at a total of 256. But from the small space in front, that is the river [illegible], the inner gates had not evidently advanced bastions. This supposition reduces the total of the gate towers to 242, which leaves a remainder of 328 to be distributed at the rate of five or six in the intervening spaces between the gates, which numbered 64. As to protection of the city, the Ganges was on the north, [illegible] on the west and south, and a [illegible] on the east.

Megasthenes' Palibothra.

In the beginning of the third century, a Chinese [illegible] describes the city as fortified, in which the king resided, and watered by streams, which flowed on all sides and

* See Plate I [illegible].

[illegible] the deep [illegible] which surrounded it. ... the palaces and [illegible] buildings were ornamented [illegible] and had inscriptions to distinguish them. The [illegible] houses were also several stories in height. The market was [illegible] by a winding street, one [illegible] extent, the shops being arranged on both sides with appropriate signs. The [illegible] of the [illegible] says that the city had [illegible] gates, the walls being wide and high. All these are, therefore, to [illegible] of the greatness and magnificence of the capital of Magadha.

Chinese description of the city.

Hiuen Tsiang notes the size of the city as 70 *li*, which, bearing in mind the proportion of the Greek parallelogram [illegible] 10, and the topographical features of the country here, makes the length as about 30 *li* and breadth as [illegible]. Part 30 *li* is equivalent to about 6 miles; and [illegible] 2 miles; and [illegible] as stated by Megasthenes. This [illegible] that during the Chinese visit in [illegible] A.D. the river and the wooden palisade must have been destroyed, and only the ruined foundations of the inner wall—that of [illegible]—was visible. This [illegible] rampart of course included the inner citadel of Ajatasatru and [illegible]; and I beg to draw to a comparative position the different sites of the inner towns.

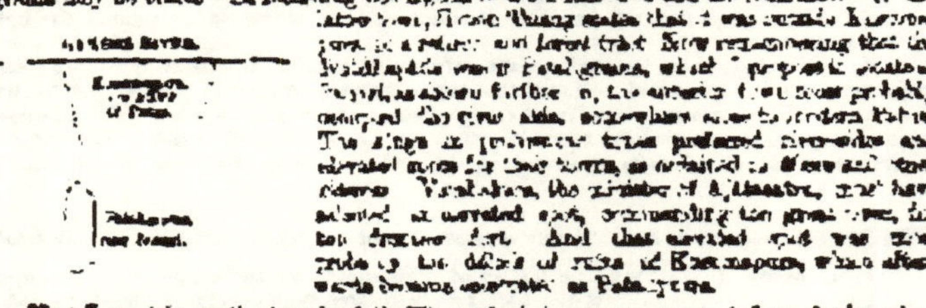

Before I take up the question of identification in detail, the relative [illegible] of the [illegible] Kusumapura and Pataliputra may be noted. In recording the legend of the Patali tree and the foundation of the latter town, Hiuen Tsiang states that it was outside Kusumapura in a [illegible] and forest tract. Now remembering that the Buddhist [illegible] was in Patali-grama, which I propose to identify [illegible], as shown further on, the [illegible] town most probably occupied this river side, somewhere near to modern Patna. The kings in prehistoric times preferred river-sides and elevated spots for their towns, as [illegible] and [illegible] Vassakara, the minister of Ajatasatru, must have selected an elevated spot, commanding the great river, for the fortress fort. And that elevated spot was most probably the débris of ruins of Kusumapura, which afterwards became converted as Pataliputra.

Clearance of the [illegible] at [illegible]

Next I [illegible] the travels of Fa Hian, which is rather easier to follow, for he gives the position and distance of the great Stupa, first constructed by Asoka, which was [illegible] south of the city. Pataliputra was one Yojana (about [illegible]) [illegible] on the [illegible] of the Ganges from the confluence of the five rivers, which I propose to identify with Barikar [illegible] (Khaturi), where the Mahanadi [illegible] is annually held and where some [illegible] (the [illegible] Sarasvati and [illegible]) are traditionally believed to have joined together (Ganges).

* [illegible] with the [illegible] confluence [illegible] Fa Hian and [illegible].

Assuming the southern rampart of the city to be somewhere near and parallel to the railway line, which must have extended to [illegible], in continuation of the [illegible] [illegible] of [illegible] [illegible] and [illegible], [illegible] more than a half mile, I [illegible] the [illegible] for the Asoka stupa at [illegible], where, on the south of the [illegible] village, is a great stupa in ruins, which was destroyed partly in the excavations of [illegible]. This important point being determined, the adjacent monuments, which were [illegible] by [illegible] of which the [illegible] [illegible] now [illegible], which [illegible] their [illegible], are not difficult to trace.

The great and [illegible] stupa of Asoka and the [illegible].

I can now take up the [illegible] of Hiuen Tsiang along with that of Fa Hian, and follow them together (see Plate I. for a restored map of Pataliputra). The great stupa of Asoka, which was in the [illegible] of the royal precincts, was in a ruinous condition; its foundation having sunk, it was leaning [illegible]. The [illegible] [illegible] of the stupa, however, as [illegible] it was made of carved stone and had a surrounding balustrade. By the side of this stupa was the [illegible] [illegible] which Fa Hian says was "very imposing and elegant." Near this was a [illegible] [illegible] to the [illegible] sect (little vehicle). Both the Sangharamas contained about [illegible] of grave and [illegible] aspect each having the proper share [illegible]. Hiuen Tsiang does not mention [illegible] from which fact I take that they were in [illegible] ruins at his time (see [illegible] and Kumrahar.

Inscribed [illegible].

To the north of the Stupa [illegible] was an inscribed pillar, [illegible] or [illegible] in girth and [illegible] in height, which recorded the giving away of the kingdom by Asoka and redeeming it with money three times. Hiuen Tsiang's *Life*, however, states that the [illegible] pillar was in the [illegible] of the Vihara, which seems to me likely to be correct. The inscription was in a mutilated condition.

Foot-prints and Vihara.

In front of the great Stupa Hiuen Tsiang says "by its side and not far from it", was the Buddhapada, enshrined in a Vihara, of which the door faced towards the north, and which Asoka appears to have built near the royal precincts; for Hiuen Tsiang says that he enclosed the stone, the footprint with the impression. The stone was 18 inches long by 6 inches broad, having still the traces of the two feet, with the wheel sign and the ten toes, all fringed with the scrolls of flowers and fishes, which glisten brightly in the morning sun. Hiuen Tsiang's *Life* adds that there was the Lotus, [illegible], and on each of the toe [illegible] was the mark of the swastika [illegible], flowers, [illegible], fish, &c. The tradition was that the Buddha stood on this stone while looking towards Magadha for the last time, and left the impression of his feet. Subsequent to the period of the Mauryas, the kings of the [illegible] tried to carry it away. "Lately Sasanka Raja," says Hiuen Tsiang, "when he was overthrowing and destroying the law of the Buddha, [illegible] to deface the sacred marks and to throw it in the Ganges (?), but it came back to its old place," that is to say, it was brought back again by [illegible] the Buddhists.

By the side of the Kukkutapada was a stupa where the four past Buddhas, previous to the [illegible], walked and sat down. As there is a [illegible] stupa still existing about a furlong to the north of the great stupa called Bari Pahari, and just south of the [illegible] village of Chhoti Pahari, [illegible] from the smaller stupa [illegible], I propose to identify it with that of the four past Buddhas. If this identification holds good, then the Kukkutarama [illegible], the Vihara, and the [illegible] must be in the immediate neighbourhood of and between the two stupas of Bari and Chhoti Paharis, which are a long [illegible] of elevated tract, extending north to south. [illegible] of Bari Pahari is a [illegible] piece of lower height, on which the village now stands. North of this, again, the elevated tract is not occupied with any houses. The village of Chhoti Pahari extends [illegible] of the [illegible], [illegible] height, though less than that of the [illegible], now known as [illegible]. About [illegible] feet north and a little east of this stupa is another high mound, crowned by a [illegible] of Musalman's [illegible]. This tract, therefore, appears to be a very promising field for excavation and discovery of ancient monuments.

I may note in passing that Dr. Waddell, seeing a [illegible] at [illegible] some [illegible] marks of the [illegible] named Bhikhnapahari as the original site of the Kukkutarama, which the bearings and distances of the Chinese pilgrims do not corroborate.

Fa Hian says that [illegible] paces north of the pagoda (Kukkutapada Vihara?) was the town of Nili or Nilas, where Asoka was born, and which he rebuilt. He raised in the [illegible] of it a stone pillar with a lion capital and about [illegible] feet in height (Legge says "more than [illegible] feet"), and inscribed on its face the [illegible] of the [illegible] and [illegible] connected with Nili, with the [illegible] year, month and day. Hiuen Tsiang does not mention [illegible]. If [illegible] the pagoda as the great stupa of Asoka, then the village of Chhoti Pahari might be the site of the old palace. But the area here is too small for a royal palace. But if the pagoda is taken to mean the Vihara of the Kukkutapada, then Nili or Nilas must be looked for at Kumrahar, where still exists a tradition of the palace of [illegible] Nand, and where, on the north, west and south, I have brought to light extensive buildings, most probably the [illegible] of the palace, which itself [illegible] under the village proper. This [illegible] must be [illegible] from being [illegible] all bearings from the old palace, which I [illegible] to be that of Nilas. Now the present name of Kumrahar [illegible] meaning, Kumrahar, the [illegible] of the [illegible], about which a tradition [illegible] Nanda. [illegible] of [illegible] to [illegible] was not a difficult process in the [illegible] of the [illegible] pronunciation in the course of ages, the inference may not be [illegible] if I take [illegible] as the [illegible] of Nilas.

Besides the palace of Nili, Fa Hian mentions another in the middle of the city, which was built of stone and carved wonderfully [illegible]. But Hiuen Tsiang appears to notice only one palace, from which he gives the bearings of the other monuments. He does not, it seems, mention the city palace, which, according to the Mudra Rakshasa, a political drama on the attainment of the throne by Chandragupta and Chanakya, was called Suganga Prasada, adorned with lofty towers and [illegible] to the river.

To the north of the old palace was an [illegible] stone-pillar, marking the site of Kalasoka's "hell," or "earth-prison," by which I understand it to be a big jail. It was a large and square space, enclosed with high walls, with a strong and wide gate, within which was a flower and fruit garden, and provided with good [illegible] and beautiful [illegible]. The [illegible] was a [illegible] who used to [illegible] persons, and wanted to [illegible] a [illegible], who was, however, miraculously [illegible]. This [illegible] Kalasoka [illegible] at once [illegible] the "hell" [illegible], after which he [illegible]. In the [illegible] of the village of [illegible] between two [illegible] Kalla and [illegible], I [illegible], along with [illegible] brick [illegible], [illegible] of [illegible] pillar, of which I [illegible] no [illegible]. It may [illegible] be [illegible] that [illegible] the "hell" of Kalasoka.

To the south of the old palace, but south of the "hell," was a great stone with a hollow [illegible], which was said to have been [illegible] by the [illegible] the [illegible] of the [illegible]. By [illegible] I understand the Yakshas of [illegible] were [illegible] to the [illegible], [illegible] the [illegible] [illegible], as recorded by Taranath, the Tibetan historian.

To the south of the old palace was a large stone house, which looked outside like a great hill, and inside many [illegible] of [illegible] wide. [illegible] the [illegible] of the [illegible]. This was the [illegible] of the King's brother, Mahendra [illegible] Vitasoka, which was built by Asoka through the agency of the genii, and probably after the model of the Gridhrakuta hill at Rajagriha. At the base of the mountain, a rock-chamber, [illegible] feet in length, 25 feet wide and [illegible] feet high, was formed with five large and square stones. Legge says [illegible] x [illegible] x [illegible] [illegible]. The spirits were said to have made a great stone [illegible] by piling up the stones, which they had brought at the King's invitation as four seats in the royal [illegible]. From the [illegible] of [illegible] to the King's half-brother, I [illegible] that [illegible]

[illegible], who was sent to Ceylon, was meant. I take him to be Vitasoka, the brother of [illegible], who rebelled against his brother and then turned a great saint in [illegible].

By the old palace, Hiuen Thsang presumably meant that of Nanda, for he does not give any hints as that we should go to the city to look for it. About three furlongs north of Kumrahar is a very large mound, on which the Dargah of Shah Arzani now stands, and at the south of which is a [illegible], still remembered as Mahendru. I propose to identify this Dargah as the ancient site of Mahendra's hermitage (see Plate V for the position of the Dargah). Here were stone relics, consisting of tall posts, a finely carved pillar with shell characters, a few winged lions of the conventional style, and some human statues, have been found. There is also said to be a stone chamber, underneath the graveyard, which extensively covers this mound. Dr. Waddell in his monograph on Asoka's classic capital, supposed the Dargah to be the city palace.

With great ingenuity, Dr. Waddell philologically argued that since Bhikna Pahari, which is more than a mile north-west of the Kumrahar palace, means evidently the hill of the Bhikshu (monk), Mahendra's hermitage must have been here; moreover as a so-called model of the Chaitya, which was originally at the top of the big mound, is now worshipped by the low-class people as Bhikna Kunwar, the monk-prince. It is now a short distance [illegible] of the mound. But the identification of El Dargah as Mahendra's [illegible] Hiuen Thsang's bearings. The Mound Mahendru is closer to the Dargah than to the Bhikna pahari, which did not yield any stone relics in my excavation.

To the south-west of the old palace was a little hill, in the crags and surrounding valleys of which were several tens of stone dwellings, which Asoka Raja [illegible] constructed for Upagupta and other Arhats by the intervention of the Yakshas. There is no elevated spot or mound south-west of Kumrahar, except a very insignificant one at [illegible], which can not serve the purpose of my identification. But if I take the south-west for simply west, then the mounds of Bahadurpur, which abounds with rough brown stones, exactly coincides with the description; for here are [illegible] and a central tank known as [illegible], which might represent the remains of the ancient crags and valleys. On the slopes of the big mound there were, I presume, small caves or cells faced with stones. The [illegible] during the early ages compelled the inhabitants to construct their houses on high mounds, which they found available in their settlement and which they selected for the purpose, so that the highest flood could not reach them. This is the reason why the Chinese pilgrims mentioned the mounds of ancient debris as mountains, still now known as Pahari, Panch Pahari, Chhoti Pahari, Bari Pahari, Bhikna Pahari.

[illegible]

By the side of the hermitage of Upagupta was an old tower (stupa) the ruins of which was a mass of irregular stones, and near which was a tank held sacred by the people, who used to bathe there to wash away their sins. The pond, which they called the "sacred water," exhibited gentle ripples, which proved [illegible]. Here Kundwa in the centre of the village might be the sacred tank; [illegible]. In that case, the [illegible] might be the [illegible] of the [illegible] stupa, where I partially excavated and found some brick remains. If the Kundwa and [illegible] do not hold good, then about a furlong north of Bahadurpur is another village known as Rampur, on the south and south-west of which are two small tanks. I have partly excavated there and exposed ancient remains, chiefly wooden. Since the northern tank has undoubtedly a drain underneath its bed, it cannot be the sacred tank. But the south-western one, called Pan [illegible] (literally meaning full of water), was evidently held in esteem in ancient days, for here the slopes are [illegible] up with brick walls, and the bed made pucca by the pavement of square bricks, below which I brought to light a grand wooden structure of the ancient period. This tank might then be the identical pond; so is the stupa the high [illegible] which is just north of the village, and underneath which I traced remains of stones and bricks, might be its representative. There is a large tank, called [illegible], south of the Dargah Arzani, which Dr. Waddell seems to think as the sacred pond of Hiuen Thsang, but it does not fully answer to the description given by the pilgrim.

[illegible]

To the south-west of the mountain, that is, the hermitage of Upagupta, [illegible] of Bahadurpur, was a collection of five stupas which at a little distance looked like little hills, and of which the lofty foundations were in ruins. These five stupas were said to be [illegible] built by Asoka [illegible] of relics, [illegible] of the five spirits, [illegible] of the Buddha. Some held them to be the treasures of Nanda Raja, which subsequently [illegible]. On the south-west of Bahadurpur is a garden, known by the name of Kankar Bagh, [illegible]. Here are two [illegible], large and small. The smaller, [illegible], covered [illegible] the stupa form, about 400 feet south-west of which, and at [illegible], is a third, near which was found, year before last, a carved architrave of the Maurya period. The first and the larger [illegible] are [illegible] into a rectangular plan for the purpose of a graveyard. This probably represents the ruins of three stupas, the other two of [illegible] are lost.

[illegible]

To the south-east of the old city was the Kukkutarama, which was built by Asoka Raja, as a sort of first fruit and a pledge of majestic [illegible] and later building, when he became a believer in the doctrines of the Buddha. In the [illegible] (Mitra's [illegible], volume II, page 40[illegible]), Kukkuta-Vihara is referred to as in a garden, called [illegible], on the right bank of the Ganges, near the city of Pataliputra. This monastery was built in ruins probably since 400 A.D., when Asoka's palace [illegible], but the foundation wall existed at the time of Hiuen Thsang's visit. By the side of the [illegible] was a great stupa,

Amalaka stupa.

called Amalaka, crowned with [illegible], which was [illegible] in India. Asoka built this stupa, when he recovered from a long sickness as a mark of gratitude to the [illegible], who blessed him at the time his majesty presented an Amalaka fruit, the only article he possessed at the time of his poverty.

North-west of the Amalaka was another stupa, known as "[illegible] the Ghanta," in commemoration of striking the bell, after twelve years

Ghanta stupa.

silence, by Aryadeva, who defeated the heretics of the Tirthika sect. This Ghanta stupa was in the middle of an old Sangharama. To the north of it was the old foundation of a ruined house, where a Brahman under the influence of a spirit, and within a curtain, used to defeat all learned men, until Asvaghosha, versed in the three vehicles, little, great and middle, silenced him.

I have not yet found an opportunity to examine the mounds on the north and east of Patna, recently under water, where [illegible] the above ruins lie imbedded in the soil. I have heard of some mounds and [illegible] of ancient [illegible] called [illegible], which are deep under soil at [illegible], and which [illegible] when [illegible] working [illegible].

Leaving the south-west corner of the city and going about 200 li paces, in the French translation, Hiuen Thsang saw an old ruined Sangharama, by the side of which was a stupa, that was held so sacred that people from far and near used to come and pray here. There were also traces of the four past Buddhas. [illegible] proposes to correct the 200 li as 200 paces from the south-west angle of the city. If it is so, then I can easily identify the remains at [illegible], where I brought to light some remains of a large terrace, stone railings, an Asoka Maurya pillar, and some remains of brick buildings. But if [illegible] is taken as the south-west corner of the old Pataliputra, as evidenced from the wooden remains, then [illegible] will mark well for the location of the monuments mentioned by Hiuen Thsang on this side.

As to the position of the city palace, probably called Sugangas, from a good and commanding situation on the high bank of the Ganges, I at first

The so-called Sugangas of the Maurya at Patna.

inclined to Dr. Waddell's identification of [illegible] Asoka, but now I propose to identify it with Maharaja [illegible], as I know that some other and better site is sought for. I have come to know, on enquiry, that at Kasim Khan's Bagh, Sadar gali, Patna, and in the Terrace of Meerza Muhammad Kaim and Azim, is an Asoka (Maurya) pillar, several feet below the courtyard, which, when opened two years ago, was so thick that two men, joining their hands together, could not measure its girth. Along with the pillar were the remains of a wooden structure in which the oil [illegible] were laid. [illegible], then it is natural to suppose that the king, who raised [illegible] pillars everywhere, even at the birth-place of [illegible], where he was born, must have erected one to heighten the importance of his city palace. I suspect that the palace site might be traced by us in the Sadar gali, presumably the high road of the ancient city.

Mr. McCrindle, in his translation of Megasthenes' Indika, page 206, states that "During the cold season of 1876, while digging a tank in Shah Mithi Wal's, a part of Patna, almost equally distant from the Chauk (kotwali) and the railway station, the excavators, at a depth of some 12 or 15 feet below the present surface, discovered the remains of a long brick wall running from north-west to south-east. How far this wall extended beyond the limits of the excavation, probably more than a hundred yards, it is impossible to say. Not far from the wall and almost parallel to it was found a line of palisades, the strong timber of which it was composed, inclined slightly towards the wall. In one place there appeared to be a sort of outlet, for two wooden pillars rising to a height of 8 or 9 feet above what had evidently been the ancient level of the place, and between which no palisade could be discovered, had all the appearance of door or gate posts. A number of wells and sinks were also found, their mouths being indicated by heaps of fragments of broken mud vessels. From the best preserved specimens of these it appeared that their shape must have differed from that of those now in use. One of the wells having been cleared out, it was found to yield capital drinking water, and, among the rubbish taken out of it, were discovered several spear-heads, a fragment of a large vessel, &c." (page [illegible].)

This palisade and brick wall at Shah Mithi Wal's might have formed the southern boundary of the imperial buildings, which must have been very extensive. There are several elevated spots and high grounds in and near Patna, which are promising fields for excavation. That the palace must have been somewhere here will be evident from what [illegible] says in his "Legend of [illegible],"

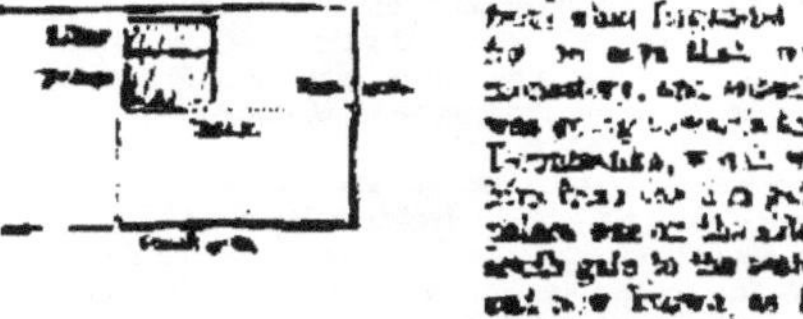

for he says that [illegible], coming from [illegible] monastery, and entering the city through the northern gate, was going towards the eastern gate to see his [illegible] at [illegible], which was to the east of Pataliputra, Asoka saw him from the [illegible] gate of his palace. This shows that the palace was on the side of the road, which passed from the north gate to the eastern one. The site north-west of Patna, and now known as [illegible], was evidently the [illegible] of the [illegible] palace, where most probably Asoka [illegible] and [illegible] constructed the first [illegible]. In the [illegible] account of the third century A.D. a [illegible], one [illegible], which forms the [illegible], applies to the present [illegible], on the north of which presumably was the palace.

CHAPTER II.—EXCAVATIONS.

The sites where I excavated from December 1896 to the [illegible] week of June 1897, with the exception of [illegible], when I was deputed to the [illegible] Tank, were Kumrahar, Nawabada, [illegible]bagh, [illegible] and [illegible], [illegible], Lohanipur, Jaganath [illegible] and [illegible]. Of these, Kumrahar had the largest share of my attention, and [illegible] I did a greater amount of [illegible] than in any other site.

The chief sites of my excavations.

On [illegible] the grounds at Kumrahar, I saw [illegible] of walls on the south bank of the Kalu Talao and on the west bank of [illegible] tank. The site between these two tanks is proposed by me to be identified with the [illegible] of Kukkutarama. On commencing excavations at these places on [illegible] December 1896, I succeeded in exposing, before long, the remains of ancient walls, which I at once followed up. By the end of February, I cleared, at Kalu tank, [illegible] feet east to west and about [illegible] feet north to south and about [illegible] feet deep, and thus brought to light a series of rooms or rather cells, on the south of which was a wall [illegible] about [illegible] feet [illegible] inches in breadth (see Plates VII and VIII for plan and sections). The cells are about [illegible] feet north to south, and between [illegible] feet [illegible] inches and [illegible] feet east to west. The breadth of the walls is about [illegible] feet, composed of single bricks set [illegible]. [illegible] brick being 1 foot [illegible] inches long by 1 foot broad, and between [illegible] and [illegible] inches in thickness. The thicker bricks were used in larger numbers. The thicker bricks are seen in the western walls, which appear to me to be the more ancient. [illegible] openings were found in the [illegible], I conclude that these were accessible from the roof, in the same way as was discovered in the [illegible] of Sultanganj. Below the foundation wall, I discovered a large fragment of a Maurya pillar, about 3 feet in diameter. I also found several smaller fragments, especially on the floor of the western cells, which appear to have been paved with them. This fact shows that this structure must have been built after the destruction of the pillar. The [illegible] of some of the [illegible] walls are bent towards the tank, which proves the pre-existence of the tank, subsequently known as the Kalu Talao, presumably from a Muhammadan [illegible].

Cells on Kalu tank.

Fragments of an Asoka pillar.

On my [illegible] from [illegible]ganj, I [illegible] the excavation, following the walls towards the south, where I had [illegible] before that they penetrated further. And on the west I [illegible] to dig near a wall in the garden, where I [illegible] some masonry exactly in line with the western wall of the exposed building. But the proprietor did not permit me to do so. This [illegible] part of the remains, therefore, is still unexplored.

Continuing the excavations on the south of the tank (see Plate IX), I found the more ancient portion of the monument; for here the walls were thicker and the foundations were about [illegible] feet below the present level of the ground. The bricks, also, showed great age by their very reddish colour, and some of them were of greater dimensions than even the larger ones mentioned before. At right angles to the series of cells so far as I exposed, and on its western wall, I traced a second series of rooms of better construction towards the south, for a length of [illegible] feet, the main wall having cross walls which branched off towards the west. Here I found a narrow passage, between two walls, about [illegible] feet 1 inch and 3 feet [illegible] inches in breadth. It is [illegible] feet [illegible] inches south of the northern range of cells. East of this narrow passage is a set of flight of steps, made of large bricks. Here also fragments of the Asoka pillar were found. The rooms were of greater dimensions than the northern cells, of which the walls extended towards the garden, where I was not allowed to dig. A copper coin, belonging to Chandra Gupta II, [illegible] type, with a peacock on the reverse, was found here.

Forty-seven feet south of the excavated area described above, and one place, and west of a dilapidated Muhammadan tomb, called Mai [illegible], I traced other walls, going farther south and west. On the south of the tomb I dug, about 18 feet deep, an area of [illegible] feet east to west, and 40 feet or so north to south. Seeing a wall which is at right angles to others here, going underneath the tomb, I [illegible] a tunnel and followed it up to its termination, [illegible] the [illegible] of the grave. In this tunnel I found several fragments of the Asoka pillar. But as the area of the trench [illegible] these fragments increased in number and size, of which [illegible] were between [illegible] and [illegible] feet in length and diameter. Below a stratum of [illegible] soil, of reddish soil and about [illegible] feet deep, I came across a layer of [illegible] earth, [illegible] ashes, embers, and bits of [illegible], between [illegible] and [illegible] feet in depth. In this [illegible] stratum the stone fragments of the pillar were invariably found (see [illegible] plate [illegible]). I then began [illegible] the black stratum at the sides of the pit I had dug, especially towards the north and the east, and brought to light innumerable fragments, large and small. In the northern [illegible] I alighted on a heap of the stone fragments, of which some were more than [illegible] feet in height and diameter. The polished surface of all these fragments looked quite fresh and new. But no inscribed portion could I discover after all my attempts to search,—which has reminded me that the Chinese pilgrims did not mention the present pillar as inscribed.

Other Asoka walls and Asoka pillar.

The fact of these pillar fragments being invariably found between a layer of [illegible] soil below a reddish stratum, more or less [illegible] feet in depth, proves that the pillar might have most probably been destroyed by [illegible] round it fuel, dry leaves and grass to a great height, which were set on fire. The [illegible] fell off in pieces and fragments, the [illegible] being burnt to lime, a slow, inexpensive, but effective way of destruction, resorted to by a vandal [illegible] of antiquity, most probably [illegible] King of Karna Suvarna, whom Hiuen Tsiang mentions as invading Magadha and breaking down Buddhist monuments.

Asoka's [illegible] from [illegible] by fire.

[illegible] Talao.

On the west of the Chaman Talao is a high mound of ancient débris, now covered with Muhammadan graves (Plate X). I began digging on the bed of the last year's excavation, and before long traced two parallel walls which extended eastward [illegible] the mound, and which I have [illegible] by tunnelling to a length of about 30 feet (Plate XI). The two parallel walls, of which about 20 feet I traced, appear to have formed an ancient drain 1 foot [illegible] in breadth, through which the sewage of the neighbouring buildings must have flowed, for I found black soil between them. Above these two parallel walls I found two others, or rather two edges of one wall, 4 feet 8 inches in thickness, which appears to have been constructed after the drain was destroyed and forgotten. And subsequently, when the latter was again in ruins, bricks were taken out by some village vandals of old. Since then, débris and earth have accumulated to a height of about 15 feet. This fact shows the great age of even this latter wall. Here also the lower wall showed better masonry.

Stupa.

Thinking the mound to be the remains of a stupa—for a carved [illegible] of a Buddhist railing was found here—I explored [illegible] on the southern slope. Going down 15 feet, I discovered some walls and a sort of small drain, round a curved wall which I took to be the foundation of the ancient stupa. Near it a chain, or something like it, was traced. I could not, however, continue this interesting discovery, for the Muhammadans objected to my so doing. Knowing that their graves did not go beyond 6 feet below the surface, I sprang a tunnel about 12 feet below and towards the north. On the northern slope also, I dug a pit, whence another tunnel was pushed on to meet the southern one. I succeeded in doing so after a month of hard labour by four diggers. Midway I traced a wall; but the whole length is [illegible] of [illegible] bricks, of which the bottom I could not reach. I am certain, however, that the most promising structure remains untouched about 15 feet below. A very interesting find is that of a [illegible] in terracotta, and a large number of [illegible] were brought out from this tunnel.

Terrace.

On the east side of the mound was cleared a terrace, about 6 feet below the top, which [illegible]. And on the east about 60 feet from the mound, Mr. [illegible] had traced another terrace before I came here: it was 6 feet below the field. South of the mound, I cleared a third terrace, near the fragment of a carved [illegible]-stone, which is under a big tamarind tree. On the east of the terrace and in the garden of the Muhammadan [illegible] I dug deep and cleared, 12 feet below the level of the ground, a wall 6 feet long by 4 feet 8 inches wide, of which the bricks were 1' 2" × 10" × 3", and which appeared to be of the most ancient period and style. About 150 feet north-east of this wall, I cleared a large space to expose a terrace, of which I could not find out the limits. In this locality a very interesting statue of the Maurya style was discovered about 40 years ago (Plate L); it is a double figure of Maya devi, carved back to back on a post of probably a Buddhistic structure, of which the two other sides show delineations of trees, [illegible], and [illegible]. The attitude of both the figures is similar, gracefully standing, and holding by their right hand the branch of a tree. It is now worshipped as Bhagavati by the villagers at [illegible], about two furlongs west of [illegible]. There being no mortise holes of the horizontal bars on all the sides, I infer that it did not belong to a Buddhist railing, but might have most probably served the purpose of a post to place offerings on in front of a Buddha statue in a temple (Vihara) which must have stood somewhere near the Chaman Talao.

[illegible] Devi.

About 500 feet west of the Chaman mound is another of larger size, which is also covered with Muhammadan graves. As it appeared to be very promising, I dug pits at its northern and western sides and wanted to clear some trenches about 15 feet [illegible] the [illegible] of graves. But the local Muhammadans raised great objections, and all my tact failed to secure the necessary permission. I had, therefore, to give up this work.

[illegible] of the palace of [illegible]

On the west of the village, [illegible] of [illegible], I carried on extensive excavations and brought to light a large number of ancient edifices, which from their depth and style of masonry appeared to be of two periods. The more ancient structures, being of better masonry, were found between 12 to 20 feet below the present level of the fields, while those of comparatively later antiquity were found about 5 feet below. These ruins appeared to be the old houses of the palace of [illegible], where Asoka was born, and which must probably occupied the site of the present village.

Commencing my description from the west, the first vestige of antiquity that came to view in a [illegible], was a long wall 4' 8" broad and about 60 feet long, so far as I followed it. Its foundation was about 16' 0" below the present level of the soil. It turned towards the south; but I could not go further for want of means. About 100 feet north of this wall, vestiges of another wall ran [illegible] in a [illegible], and 150 feet or so east of it. A third was detected in a sound state, which I at once ordered to be [illegible] up at a short distance from it, in order not to damage it in any way. Going 12 feet down, I cleared a wall of the most ancient style, which showed better shape in a wall, and which extended north to south. Tracing it northward for about 40 feet from the wall, I came across, on the north of the footpath, another wall 4' 8" wide, which extended eastward, 264 feet further east, and on the north of the footpath a third wall was traced, which went from west-south-west to east-north-east.

On the [illegible] (? [illegible]), and about 275 feet east of the last excavation near the well, I brought to light extensive buildings, of which a wall, 7' 6" broad, was traced to a length of 130 feet east to west (see Plates XII, XIII, for plan and sections). At both of its ends several cross walls were found, going north to south. The eastern cross walls, three in [illegible], showed deeper foundation and presented masonry of a better style, apparently of the more ancient period. The [illegible] or [illegible] cells, which were on the east end of which there was apparently [illegible], were about 8' 9" x 7' 6" in length and breadth. Just on the west side of them, I found a narrow passage, like the one on the north-east of the Mokarbal. About 35 feet south-west of the last excavation, I cleared another spot and brought to light the remains of a [illegible] edifice, of which the eastern portion appeared to be a stair, 11' 6" broad, which was constructed of very large bricks. A wall [illegible] from it towards the north, west of which, but not parallel, runs a [illegible] wall, built in similar bricks.

About 40 feet east of the stair, another edifice was found, of which two walls about three feet wide, and at right angles to each other, extended north and east-north-west. One of the walls showed [illegible] [illegible] in a [illegible], peculiar to the style of the Maurya architecture. From the meeting point of the two walls, that is to say, from the corner of the ancient [illegible], extended a [illegible] wall of smaller bricks and undoubtedly of [illegible] age. On the south of these remains and at a spot [illegible] with a [illegible] in the place, I [illegible] a large [illegible] in horizontal [illegible], of which the [illegible] is not seen in the [illegible] of [illegible]. About 15 feet further east, I [illegible] an old wall stone masonry about 12 feet below the ground, and on digging a deep pit at a short distance from it, found some brick steps and a portion of another wall in front of it. A quantity of small [illegible] stone was also exposed on the south face of the pit.

Returning to the western end of the main wall, 7' 6" broad, which was [illegible] [illegible], three parallel cross walls were [illegible] out at no great depth from the surface. Continuing my excavations westward, a wall three feet wide was traced to a length of 73 feet or so. This wall, with the [illegible] ones, east to west, was of very good masonry and appeared to be of the highest antiquity. At its northern end and on the east side was a room about 7' 6" in span; and, to the south and towards the west, some three or four were discovered, which were not, however, fully cleared. The bricks were of very large size and became [illegible] with great age. The foundation of the wall here was found 15 feet or so below the present level of the fields. Mr. J. A. Bourdillon, the Commissioner, who came one fine morning of June last, was surprised to see the large number of ancient [illegible], and exclaimed that the excavated area [illegible] the site of Patna and its [illegible].

On the [illegible] of the village of [illegible], brick masonry was [illegible] [illegible] near an old well called [illegible] [illegible], and about 20 feet below the present level of the fields (see Plate XIV for plan and sections and Plate XIV for two [illegible]). In this neighbourhood, Mr. [illegible] had excavated in the hot season of 1896 and found a large amount of ancient [illegible] (shells). I began excavating in January 1897, a short distance north of the well, and before ten feet depth was reached, a small cell, six feet square, was exposed to view. Clearing it all round, a terrace was found, south of the cell, being five feet below the level of the field. Five feet lower still, and a little eastward, I was glad to discover a fragment of a Maurya pillar, near which a great number of small cylindrical bricks, 1 foot 6 inches long by 7 or 8 inches in diameter, and somewhat strangely [illegible] laid, were brought to light. These finds made me [illegible] to look in the immediate neighbourhood for some important monuments, to which these peculiar bricks must have belonged, and which, however, I could not discover. Before I lighted on these finds, I [illegible] another cell just north of, and attached to, the other. The eastern wall of both the cells turned out to be quite a curve, sloping outwards as it went down. This observation led me to conclude that this might have been the portion of a bastion, most probably belonging to the royal palace, which existed in this neighbourhood. To trace this supposed bastion, I dug deep on the north-east of the curved wall, where I found it broken and destroyed [illegible] [illegible], no Asoka fragment, and the cylindrical bricks mentioned above. And so I stopped excavating below 17 feet, but continued [illegible] at the foundation of the first discovered cell, which I [illegible] [illegible] a thick layer of broken pottery, at least 18 feet [illegible] below the present level of the ground. As to the terrace, I could not [illegible] it [illegible], as there were crops standing at the time. But towards the east and north of the pit, I traced other walls, as shown in plan. The two cells appeared to be two inner walls [illegible]. As to the cylindrical bricks, Mr. [illegible], the Chief Engineer, who saw my collection of relics in December last, suggested that they might have served the purpose of coping to walls.

I heard that at a short distance north-east of the two cells above-mentioned, and in the compound of a [illegible] house, there is a subterranean passage which leads to several rooms, all now lying deep under the earth. My impression is that these remains might most probably belong to the royal palace, which I was in search of so long. But time and funds did not allow me to undertake this promising work.

In a [illegible]'s house ([illegible]) on the east of the village, I excavated a small area down to 20 feet, and found some remains of walls and terraces. The stratum of [illegible], here as elsewhere, was found to be formed of a [illegible] debris of broken bricks, generally 12 feet in depth, below which I expected some remains of ancient monuments. In another [illegible]'s house, I saw two walls going eastward; but I did not find time and means to dig here.

About 100 feet west of the double wall or reservoir, a cultivator, in digging a well in his fields, got out in pieces a quantity of ancient wood, which I thought to be the remains of an ancient palisade. It was found in a stratum of black and [illegible] soil, which is [illegible] to deep [illegible] as that of the [illegible]. But I did not get an opportunity to dig and examine it.

Pataraya.

Midway between the double villages of Panch [illegible] and Kumrahar, and about 2 furlongs south-east of the latter, is a high and large mound, known as Pataraya [illegible] ([illegible] meaning mound) which is on the north of a marsh of the same name, Pataraya [illegible] [illegible] from a large number of graves, which are found in this mound and of the Pirs and Fakirs. It is also [illegible] here, covered with Muhammadan graves. In the month of May, I ordered a small party of diggers to excavate it on its tops on the east, south and west. In a few days I was glad to discover an interesting image of Mahadeva in polished black stone with its Argha or receptacle, about 5 feet below the surface of the eastern slope and over a wall. Going further down, some walls were traced. On the western side also some thick walls of the ancient town were found, about 15 feet below the top (see Plate II & XV).

On the north of the village of Panch [illegible], I detected some thick walls in the fields, and about two furlongs east of the same village, the remains of a wooden palisade were noticed deep in a well. But [illegible] [illegible] [illegible] [illegible] appeared to be the most promising; the two [illegible] the two Stupas, two monasteries, a [illegible] temple and an inscribed pillar of Asoka, which [illegible] and [illegible] visited by the Chinese pilgrims, led me to extend [illegible]. The two Stupas are [illegible] still [illegible] high [illegible], which Dr. Waddell [illegible] excavated and failed to identify.

Trench driven in the centre of the two Stupas at Pahari in 1898.

On the mound at Bari Pahari, which I believe to be the two Stupas erected by Asoka, the trench, [illegible] 72 and then 30 feet wide and 25 feet long, was commenced on 8th October 1898 (see Plate XV). It was driven directly to the north-east to the very centre of the solid brickwork, where the trench was widened to 40 by 34 feet. It was then carried down to a depth of 27 feet, and the centre sunk to 40 feet, where water prevented further [illegible]. But nothing of archæological interest was brought to light. The excavation of the mound at Chhoti Pahari brought to light the core of the solid brickwork, more than 60 feet in diameter, which I propose to identify with the Stupa of the four past Buddhas mentioned by Hiuen Tsiang. It appears that the bricks from the centre, where presumably was the relic chamber, were removed several centuries ago by the Muhammadan [illegible] of [illegible] [illegible] subsequently the hollow was filled up with rubbish [illegible] to form a platform for the purpose of a [illegible]. After excavating down to 30 feet, [illegible] was found [illegible] solid masonry was again dug into, 4 feet further deep. Altogether 34 feet of [illegible] Stupa was [illegible] cut down under the supervision of a [illegible] expert, without the discovery of any relics.

This vandal and destructive excavation of two important monuments, which cost above Rs. 700, should never have been allowed by an expert, who is [illegible] to be the chief archæological authority in the North-Western Provinces and Oudh. Dr. Waddell [illegible] witnessed this costly but at the same time useless excavation. But my system of proceeding is quite different. I take a sort of religious care in preserving what I expose; and I am very strict in not allowing my men to break even detached bricks, for which I suppose they had to use their spade very carefully. Thus [illegible], not one relic of the many that I brought to light has been broken. My procedure is generally to work from the centre, following the remains by the edge of the spade, but at a short distance and then gently drawing nearer, so as to avoid all chances of breakage.

Wooden structure under [illegible] tank.

In closely examining the walls in the [illegible] dry bed of the [illegible] tank, I detected in one, near the [illegible] temple (Plate XVI), the remains of some wooden structure, to open which I at once gave order in April last. Two feet below the bed of the tank, my men stopped on a layer of thick planks, spread over a bedding of brickbats and beams, of which I exposed a fragment [illegible]. The fragment of the beam has a [illegible] to receive the tenon of a post, which would have supported the ancient [illegible] or palisade. But the [illegible] [illegible], [illegible] of ages, [illegible] [illegible] [illegible], and when I [illegible] with some difficulty, and [illegible] I took out the [illegible] from amidst water which had [illegible] out [illegible] before, I had therefore to give up the attempt of following and carefully examining this wooden structure, which appeared to extend east to west. [illegible] [illegible] that I could not [illegible] the portion I exposed. I took out the [illegible] and the portion of the [illegible] that supported them, and rearranged them in the way I found them under water, as shown in the sketch. This is the only place where I [illegible] found [illegible] remains.

Sculptures [illegible] temple.

Near the temple of Sitala Devi, just north-west of the wooden structure mentioned above, is a small collection of sculptured stones, of which one is a pretty face of the Buddha and another is a fragment of a railing, and a third a [illegible] (Plate [illegible]). And in the temple of Siva, on the western bank [illegible] the [illegible] are three more fragments of a Buddhist rail which [illegible] interesting carvings. In the [illegible] medallion of one of them are [illegible] figures of Mahadeva and wife, standing in an amatory attitude. Another one shows the [illegible] figure of a man [illegible]. The Linga of Mahadeva, to which the temple is dedicated, has the head of Parvati attached to it.

Agam Kuan.

At the Agam Kuan, close to the [illegible] well, is a [illegible] female figure, carved in the style of Mayadevi at [illegible], which appears to be of the Maurya period (Plate XXVII, 3). And the big well itself.

of which the diameter is about 2½ feet, has the stamp of a great age. This female figure, which has a modern and [illegible] head is now worshipped as Sitala Devi, the Goddess of small-pox.

On the north of the railway line and of Kumrahar is an ancient canal or [illegible], starting from the south-east corner of the [illegible] tank, extends towards the west for about 2,000 feet, along the southern edge of which I traced a long wall, 3 feet or so wide and composed of the usually large-sized bricks. The bed of the canal, northward from this wall, is paved with bricks. I could not determine to what length the wall extended. Between this canal and the railway is a small plot of ground, where I heard that beams and [illegible], locally [illegible] posts, which name the villagers assign to the remains of the palisade, were found some years ago. I began to dig a pit to trace the latter; but I could not go very sufficiently deep when rain commenced and stopped my work. Between the canal and the railway I excavated a trench, about 150 feet east to west, to trace up a structure, of which I had discovered a vestige in a well. I went down to 10 feet and traced a wall, which appeared to be most ancient. And east and a little eastward, but just below the surface of the field, I traced a large amount of brick masonry which appeared to be the remains of an ancient stûpa, the bricks being placed on the edge-to-edge [illegible]. In the northern direction of the [illegible] and on the north of Kumrahar, I observed walls and masonry, which, however, I did not find time to trace.

On the east of Kumrahar, a small village of [illegible], which [illegible] ground and the fields which are on the east of the [illegible] tank are very high. Here is a collection of ancient stone figures all broken and defaced. This locality, therefore, appeared to be very promising; and so I commenced digging a long trench. But the rains prevented my digging a great length to discover anything.

North-west of Kumrahar and between the road and the railway, is a temple of the [illegible] period and a graveyard, which stand on ancient ground (Plate XVII). On the north of them and of the railway, some pits were sunk down in order to bring to view several posts of the palisade, which the villagers informed me were lying about 25 feet below the ground level. I could not go beyond 10 feet when rain stopped me. I, however, succeeded in exposing extensive buildings, both ancient and mediæval, between 5 and 10 feet below the present level of the ground. By mediæval I mean the period subsequent to the Maurya period and long antecedent to the visit of Hiuen Tsiang in 637 A.D. The characteristics of the two periods of architecture here were the same as observed at Kumrahar.

On the west of the village of [illegible] there is a large tank, apparently very ancient, and now known by the name of [illegible], who probably once repaired it along with the ghât (Plate XVIII). The ghât is just below a high mound which is covered with Muhammadan graves. It is on the eastern bank of the tank. I excavated the western face of the central one, exposed both Hindu and Muhammadan remains. The remains of the Muhammadan ghâts showed masonry of small bricks, cemented with surki (brick-dust) and lime, while the more ancient Hindu structure was made of the usual layers of very large bricks laid in mud (see Photograph XVIII(a)). The Muhammadan ghât appeared to be flanked by octagonal bastions, inside which were Hindu walls and terraces one above another. But before long I stopped this work, for just on the north side of the tank and of the road [illegible], I discovered a series of very interesting ghâts, which at once engrossed my attention for the long [illegible].

Between the railway and the road, and just beyond the northern ditch, I detected some bricks in a pit of a brick-field, and about 15 feet below (see Plate XIX for plan and sections). After clearing it to a certain extent, I found it continuous and rising in a slope. I then began to dig on the other side running parallel to the ditch and in a line with the first wall [illegible]. After a month's hard labour, I cleared out a series of small ghâts, at short distances from one another, the intervening spaces being occupied and strengthened with three parallel and massive walls, the highest, that is, the southern wall, being [illegible]. These flights of steps face towards the north, and are constructed of both horizontal and vertical layers of brick, [illegible] being flanked by [illegible] to [illegible] and strengthen it. The formation of the soil, so far as I went down, was composed of three strata: the first is [illegible] soil, about [illegible] feet deep, below which is a layer of [illegible] and [illegible] about [illegible] feet deep. Below the [illegible] stratum is [illegible] about 2 feet thick, below which again was seen the sand. Here water prevented me from going further down and so I could not open and examine the lower portion of the ghâts.

I traced this series of ghâts for a length of more than 750 feet, east to west, beyond which I did not go, but I cannot say how far it extends. Now the [illegible] is peculiar to the river side, and since the villagers in the neighbourhood remember a tradition that the Son used to flow here in ancient times, I did not find any difficulty in identifying the ghâts as belonging to that river, which then, during the Maurya period, served as the ditch of Palibothra [illegible] wall. Among these ghâts and walls, I found the fragment of the largest brick I have yet seen in the ruins of this great city.

About 500 feet south of these ghâts and the railway is a site known as [illegible], so called from its eminence. Here under a [illegible] tree was a heap of rough stone which, shown to the eyes of Dr. Waddell, were said traces of a Stûpa, and were identified by him as the very [illegible] mentioned by Hiuen Tsiang. Accordingly, on the expectation of discovering the neighbouring monuments as shown in the Doctor's pamphlet, Mr. [illegible]

[illegible] two long trenches, at right-angles to each other about [illegible] feet wide and [illegible] feet deep, and discovered a most interesting capital of the Maurya style of sculpture (Plate XLVII). It is in yellowish sandstone and very large in size, the different faces showing ornaments of honeysuckle, [illegible] and other [illegible] (see illustration). Near it was found another big [illegible] block of stone of the same kind, which appears to have been intended for another capital, but for some unknown reason was left unworked. Near it was traced some terrace made of rubble and earth on a bedding of bricks. Mr. Mills also found [illegible] copper coins, of which two were rectangular and punch-marked, one Chinese being circular with a hole in the centre, and two Muhammadan known as Madhmudi. I widened Mr. Mills' excavations, exposing other terraces and walls; but not finding very promising, I stopped this work before long.

About 1,500 feet west of the first pillar and at Dhu [illegible], I detected some wood in a [illegible] which [illegible] gave signs (Plate XL). About [illegible] feet below the soil a wooden [illegible] was exposed, standing on a [illegible] [illegible]. Above this, a thick layer of broken vessels, about [illegible] feet in depth, was cut through. And on the west a thick wall with great [illegible] and the remains of a stair were [illegible]. The large bricks were very [illegible] in colour, which showed great antiquity. There was another wall, running [illegible] and parallel to it. I could not continue this very interesting excavation, for [illegible] my funds ran short, and secondly I could not get sufficient number of coolies to work at simultaneously at some fifty places in the months of May and June.

Wooden and brick remains at [illegible].

In the garden known as Lakhan [illegible] [illegible] in December 1896 [illegible] a [illegible] mound which is covered by [illegible] graves, I succeeded in tracing some small walls, which, however, [illegible] not [illegible]. North of this mound is a large, elevated and [illegible] piece of ground, which is also covered with graves. I examined it by digging a trial trench [illegible] but [illegible] excavated did not yield any remains. About [illegible] feet south-east of the [illegible] mound is another in the [illegible] of [illegible], where Mr. Mills [illegible] had found an interesting [illegible], which is carved with ornaments [illegible]. These mounds are [illegible] by me as the site of the [illegible] stupas erected by Asoka.

Stupas at Lakhan [illegible].

About a [illegible] long [illegible] of Lakhan [illegible] is the village of [illegible], which stands on an extensive mound, and which I propose to identify as the [illegible] of [illegible]. On the west of the village is another mound, which I excavated to a considerable extent and exposed a number of rooms and walls as also some [illegible]. In the eastern [illegible] of the village, I [illegible] some wooden remains, to expose which I began to dig in June. I exposed a series of wooden posts, which most probably belonged to the same drain that Mr. Mills [illegible] and [illegible] in May 1896, midway between here and Rampur. An interesting [illegible], which was gilded with gold leaf, was found in the [illegible] of [illegible], which has [illegible] during ages. I could not make much progress, when the rains commenced and [illegible] the [illegible] between [illegible] and Rampur.

Midway between [illegible] and Rampur a cultivator informed Mr. Mills' [illegible] that there were beams underneath the land. On this information, he ordered excavation without delay in May 1896. Twelve feet below the field level, a wooden structure was seen, which, on further opening, was found to be a drain constructed with beams and posts on a bedding of bricks. All the timbers, consisting of [illegible] beams and [illegible] posts, were removed to his bungalow, of which but a few now remain. It was worse than useless [illegible] to destroy an ancient monument of undoubtedly the Maurya period, and then to burn the excavated wood as fuels for [illegible]. Mr. Mills traced the drain for a length of about [illegible] feet, when rain stopped his work. A rough drawing was made by his [illegible], which I found to be not much reliable and a tracing of which is submitted herewith.

Wooden remains at [illegible] and Rampur.

I had therefore to continue the work, when I returned from [illegible], by sinking wells at short distances, beyond the portion Mr. Mills had examined. I also dug a small pit down to about 18 feet in order to examine minutely the strata of the soil and the nature of the [illegible] [illegible]. I could not, however, find the kind of construction that he had discovered. [illegible] I found, below 18 feet, a drain 7 feet 6 inches broad and [illegible] feet high, which had two brick walls, [illegible] upward, and the bed of the [illegible] paved with bricks, [illegible] inches square (Plates XXI, XXV, for plan and section). Above the brick walls, planks of [illegible] wood (now [illegible]), between 2 and 3 inches thick, were spread on the top of the brick [illegible]. In carefully opening one plank, about [illegible] feet [illegible], I found the channel filled with black mud, the silt of ages. It gave me the greatest trouble to preserve the woods. When I exposed them, the woods looked quite fresh and new. But after a little exposure to sun and air they began to crack and split to a frightful degree. I had therefore to cover them with moist earth, after [illegible] measuring and sketching them. I traced the drain for a length of about [illegible] feet, when rain prevented my proceeding further. The drain extends south and a little west [illegible] and [illegible] a little [illegible], coming from the direction of the palisade I discovered on the [illegible] of the village of [illegible].

Drain

The portion that Mr. Mills exposed and removed was [illegible] feet long, and showed a kind of construction different from what I brought to light, being more complicated than mine (Plates XXII, XXIII, and XXIV for the plan and two sections). Stout cross-beams, [illegible], were laid across two [illegible] walls or rather [illegible] of bricks, and were supported at the sides by standing posts [illegible] feet [illegible] inches high.

and 9" in width broad and thick. The walls of the drain were also constructed of thick blocks of wood 8 inches thick and made almost water-tight by fine setting one above another. On these two walls was a roofing of wooden blocks about 1 foot in thickness, same in the same manner I discovered in the drain [illegible] at Lohanipur, described further on. The blocks of wood laid longitudinally in the walls, flooring and roofing, were between 17' × 11½" × 8" and 10' × 9" × 6" in dimensions (Plates XXVI and XXVII).

About 100 feet west of the drain is a small tank known as [illegible], in the dry bed of which I detected wood in April last (Plate XXV). On digging only a foot or two I found the remains of a wooden structure which extended from east to west, the western portion being under a pavement of bricks, where two beams were seen, of which one showed [illegible] at its western end to fit in the hole of the other. Here the earth appeared to be hard and reddish; while in the old bed of the tank the silt appeared to be black and soft. About 30 feet further west I sunk a well to trace the wooden structure as to its length. But though I went down to the water-level, about 12 feet, I did not find any remains, the soil here being quite natural. On the south of the wooden remains I found two round posts, and another further on, which were in a line with them. On clearing the embankment at the south, east and north, some sloping walls were traced out, as also a bedding of square and large bricks. Beneath the first layer of these timbers of sal, which I removed for better scrutiny, was another timber layer which we extended east to west. In this layer was one log, still standing as originally fixed, which supported the wooden wall. In the second layer of wooden remains was found an axe with which the carpenter dug out the timber for the wooden structure, which is accidentally left, and was lost.

On the north and a little west of the long drain, I detected wood in April last in the same dry bed of a tank just south of the village of [illegible] (see Plate XXVIII for plan and sections). On clearing the sandy earth, a wall of wooden planks, three inches thick, was brought to light. Going 13 feet down, and making a pit of about 20 feet square, I found the wooden structure to be of peculiar construction. Two beddings of sal timber, parallel to each other from east to west and each 1' 3" broad by about 6" thick, were placed 4' 4½" apart, on which stout posts, about one foot square, stood to strengthen and form two parallel walls of planks. The latter walls stood on an upper bedding of wood, 2' 10" above the lower, being four blocks of wood laid in a rectangle, 6' 6" by 2' 6", over which, on the north and south faces, the plank wallings were raised to a height of about 5 feet. Another plank walling was traced from the south-west corner of the structure and over the upper bedding. It extended towards the north, but how far I could not determine, it being [illegible] in [illegible] condition. West of this raised walling were found other blocks of wood which also extended north to south.

To the east and north of the rectangular structure, other beams, going north to south, and at different levels below the tank bed, were also traced. Since I cleared only a small area, I could not determine how far all these beams and beddings extended in different directions. The plan, sections, and view, herewith enclosed, will convey a better idea of the structure, which appears to be quite unique. Two axes and a nail with two points at one end were here found, about 10 feet below the tank bed. One of the axes has its hole fossilised, indicating the great age it was buried.

In tracing the long drain from near [illegible], known to the very centre of the tank bed, and only about 15 feet east of the above structure, where the deepest my work [illegible], I could not properly ascertain how it was connected with the rectangular structure or where it terminated. Here was one of the most interesting points of ancient architecture, which rain prevented me from opening and studying.

Bhikhnapahari is a very large mound, about three furlongs north-west of Kumrahar. About 250 years ago an officer of Ali Vardi Khan, the Nawab Nazim, came here and, removing the middle hill, known as, worshipped as Bhikna Kuar, which was on the top and at the north-west corner, built here his house which his descendants now occupy (see Plate XXIX). Getting permission from them with great difficulty, I excavated at four places on the west side of the mound, two along the north and another in the east. These excavations showed that the mound is very largely composed of brick rubble and débris of ancient buildings. The pit on the northern side was dug down to 8 feet, when the Nawab's people stopped my cutting further. The pit, marked B in the plan, exposed a wall, which extended north-east and south-west, 17 feet below the surface (Plate XXX). Two terraces were also traced, one 15 feet below, and the other at the middle height of the slope, of which I had detected the edge then visible. In the trench marked C, 30 feet long and 6 feet wide, I dug down to more than 18 feet, nothing was found except rubble and débris, among which an interesting brick, moved with scrolls on one face, was discovered.

The trench, marked D (see Plates XXXI and XXXII for plan and section), 40' long, 14' wide, and 17' 7" deep, was the most fruitful of architecture. From 13' 4" below the present platform of the mound two parallel walls were exposed; and going 6' 6" deeper, I cleared what appeared to be a narrow passage, 4' 3" wide and 15' 6" long, east to west. Its floor was paved, being made of concrete. On the east end the passage was shut out by a wall, beyond which I was not permitted to dig. At the western end of the passage, the floor goes down by six feet [illegible] and [illegible] westward I traced a wall of the most ancient pattern going north to south. Above the southern wall of the passage ran another wall like a step. Here below I suspected a hollow or wall, just behind the first southern wall, which, no sooner I cleared the wall, made the horizontal courses of the bricks sink down and drag out a portion of the masonry. I could not [illegible], examine the [illegible] of this [illegible] or wall. The western side of the [illegible] of the passage appears to have been [illegible] of [illegible], the broken ends of the bricks looking quite fresh, as if done yesterday. There were also the vestiges of other walls above the two passage walls, and above the western end of the southern wall I saw thick layer of earth (? [illegible]), [illegible] in a way, [illegible], I could not determine, for [illegible] was not discovered in any part of the ancient structure here.

The pit marked B was dug on the south-west corner of the [illegible]. It showed a terrace of earth and [illegible] walls going outward; I could not determine how far. The [illegible] of these walls shows some [illegible] in the plan, indicating that this structure was most probably a temple. Had I been permitted to excavate further outward, I would have struck at the main building. Here I found a terracotta figure and a [illegible].

In pit marked C, I found a wall and two [illegible] about 14 feet below an [illegible] terrace, which appears to have been constructed long after the [illegible] of the Maurya monument.

From these excavations, which were done on the slopes of the mound, it is [illegible] to expect very promising results, if the main structure be exposed, at least partially. [illegible] the century of 1857, the [illegible] excavated some deep [illegible] to hide their treasures, and struck at several walls at certain depth below the present surface of the mound. Some peculiarities of construction were found in the remains of ancient architecture [illegible].

The most [illegible] place after Kumrahar was [illegible] [illegible], where on the site of the ancient park, I found several important remains, two Maurya pillars of the Asoka style, one big terrace, a Buddhist railing and a wooden palisade with drain underneath. (See map in Plate VI and section plans in Plate XXXIII.) On the north-east of the [illegible], I [illegible] a long terrace in [illegible] which appeared [illegible] to west for about [illegible] feet. This terrace was peculiar in construction: the first layer was a bedding of brick-bats, above which was spread a layer of earth and lime (broken bricks in small fragments). Above this again was another layer of [illegible] in solid mass, [illegible] and properly [illegible]. This terrace was [illegible] 2 feet [illegible] below the present level of the field.

In exposing the terrace on the north of the [illegible], I succeeded in discovering the [illegible] [illegible] Buddhist railing of a plain style, of which five posts are still in situ, and the [illegible] below in a neighbouring well. It must have enclosed a stupa or other Buddhistic monument, which, however, I could not find. The posts were about 1' 6", more or less, were apart from one another, [illegible] in breadth and [illegible] in thickness, their upper portion being broken. I could not ascertain their original height. But from the existing portion, which is about 3' 5" in height, I can calculate it to be about 6 feet, as the [illegible] hole is 7½" high by about 5" wide, and the interval between the two [illegible], [illegible]. Now remembering that there were three horizontal bars attached to the posts, we get the total height for the [illegible] as about [illegible], and, for the whole, about 8 feet above the terrace. Of the horizontal bars, two fragments were also found, which fit in the holes at the sides of the posts. The posts were fixed about 1' [illegible] deep in the terrace above [illegible]. After sketching and taking measurements of the existing posts, which formed the north-east corner of the rail enclosure, that was [illegible], I covered them again with earth for safe custody.

About three hundred feet south-west of the railing, I cleared a pit and found the remains of houses, chiefly of the mediaeval period, about [illegible] feet below the present field level. Here I found several ancient beads and coins, [illegible] punch-marked, and one [illegible] [illegible]. Some tiles, backed with silver leaves, were also discovered, being mixed with [illegible] soil.

About 25 feet south-west of the last remains and below older remains of brick houses, I went down to about 10 feet, when I found a layer of ashes about 3" thick, which probably belonged to buildings and [illegible], and which were almost [illegible] with age. About [illegible] below this, I was glad to expose several large fragments of a Maurya pillar more than 3 feet in diameter. (Plate XXXIV.) Among them was found [illegible] a [illegible], about [illegible] feet in length. A large number of [illegible] [illegible] [illegible] pieces and highly polished, were also found [illegible]. Some of the [illegible] showed [illegible] which [illegible] struck [illegible] as [illegible] of [illegible], of which I [illegible] one broken piece here. I could not take out the big fragments of the Asoka pillar and the [illegible], and [illegible] the [illegible] of the rains, I had to fill up the pit for the purpose of [illegible].

About 200 feet west of the last pit, I made another about 12 feet deep, and was glad to alight on the top of the capital of the Asoka pillar, whose diameter is 3' 7½". On clearing it further the capital appeared to be of a [illegible] vase form, in the centre of which was a hole for the reception of the tenon of the lion or some other animal, which must have originally crowned the pillar. Innumerable fragments of it, besides the capital, were found in the pit, some of which showed ornamental bands of lotus petals and [illegible]. On the north side of the pit, I traced a wall about 8 feet below the present soil, which [illegible] northward to a length I could not determine. The base of the capital is square, being 3' 3" on each of the faces, of which one has an ornament of lotus, flowers or [illegible] [illegible] or [illegible] characters, which no scholar has yet deciphered. I succeeded in taking up the capital and other fragments with the help of the railway [illegible].

About [illegible] furlongs south of these excavations, I heard of a wooden [illegible] in the wall of a [illegible] [illegible]. (Plate XXXV for plan and section.) On going down 12' 6" below the very hard earth, which I had to cut through with some difficulty, my men alighted on the vestiges of a palisade, at the bottom of which was the drain. It extended north to south, which I followed up to a length of about 50 feet by trenching at the two sides of the pit. Two parallel lines of sal posts 1' 6" from each other, ran north to south; and the posts in each line were at equal distances from one another, the intervals being between 3' 6" and 5' 0". Against the inner face of the posts stout beams were laid [illegible] one above another to a height of about 3', to form walls of the drain, which was roofed over with long beams, 6" in thickness. This roof and the walls were supported from inside with an inner framework of timber posts and cross beams. On the east side of the drain, and 5 feet distant from it, was exposed an octagonal pillar, of which each face was 9½" × 10" in breadth. This octagonal pillar of which the upper part appeared to be turned into earth, stands on a thick plank of wood, about one foot in thickness and four feet in breadth. It extended eastward, how far I could not determine, for it was [illegible] easy to drive a [illegible] here. Just west of the octagonal pillar is one of the posts of the outer framework, the interval being only 3" at the bottom and 1' above the plane of the roof of the drain. Three smaller posts, which were 8" × 7" in section, were [illegible] 4' × 7", and east to west, with remains of planks, which prove that there was a wooden wall above the drain. On the northern end of the drain and close to it, I traced another wooden wall, which ran at right angle to the lower one, that is to say, east to west; this wall was flanked by the two [illegible] of the drain. At the southern end [illegible] of the roof I traced a third cross wall, which was very much in ruins. On the west of the drain, I saw other woods spread [illegible] in plan. This very interesting of the ancient monuments at Pataliputra was not properly examined, for rain continued during [illegible] and prevented me from further digging.

[illegible]

On the south of Lohanipur and the railway are the remains of a long wall, called [illegible], which extended a long way east to west, and parallel to the latter. This wall ought to be the remains of the ancient fort, which the villagers are still remember as the Raja's [illegible]. On the south of the road running east of the western ditch of the road going south from the railway gate, a heap of some wooden remains [illegible] the ground, which I shall try to open and examine when the next occasion arrives.

Oval plan temple of [illegible]

The mound at [illegible], on the north, east and west sides of which are very low and marshy fields, [illegible] of an ancient [illegible], looked promising at the first sight; and I commenced digging in January 1897 (See Plates XXXVI and XXXVII for plan and sections). By the end of [illegible] a large oval-planned structure was traced at only a foot or two below the surface. Its inner diameter was 60 feet, while the breadth was 35, the outer ones being respectively [illegible]. The thickness of the wall, which showed batter, was 4' 0", and the depth about 6' 0". Along the longer diameter was a wall, which divided the oval into two equal portions, and which were again subdivided into ten compartments by four cross walls. The central room was extended westward and northward beyond the outer [illegible] about 7 feet to meet two cross walls, each 4 feet 6 inches in width, which extend east to west, being limited on the west by a wall about 5 feet broad. The outward plan is thus a rectangle, of which the eastern wall I could not trace. On the eastern side, however, I brought to light some rooms and passages; and on the west of the oval there are five cross walls to partition the outer enclosed space into seven rooms. This edifice appears to be very peculiar and interesting, and its importance will be evident to the students of Fergusson's "Indian and Eastern Architecture," in which the author, in discussing the forms of the Chaitya and other caves, could not trace their origin. The circular temple, which he mentions in Southern India as originating the oval form, cannot be accepted as such on [illegible] consideration. Now considering the fact that Asoka the [illegible] of making the Buddhist faith [illegible] the state, covered the whole of India with religious monuments, this [illegible] temple might very most probably supplied the model [illegible] as the most elegant plan for the caves of Central and Western India. About 200 feet south of the existing temple are [illegible] buried in the earth, and to the north of the village of [illegible], and east of [illegible], two [illegible] were discovered in the fields.

[illegible]

The last mound, where I dug in January 1897, was the [illegible], which is at the west of the [illegible] of the ancient [illegible] now remembered by the people as [illegible]. I dug in the middle and on the north-eastern side, bringing to light some walls, which I at once followed up towards the west and the north (Plate XXXVIII for ground plan). Not only the remains of several rooms, but a good number of large jars were exposed, about 8 feet below the surface. Some terracotta [illegible] of human figures, horses, and other articles. Terracotta vessels, mostly broken, were also found, some showing graceful forms. As to stone relics, several fragments of [illegible] and pillars [illegible], worshipped by the ignorant people as [illegible] Devi, a [illegible] pedestal of a statue and a half [illegible] slab, which shows some peculiar ornaments, and the base of others in [illegible], were brought to light. On the north-east corner of the mound is an elevated spot dedicated to [illegible] Devi, which consists of a large number of old stones. Among them is a statue of [illegible], rather defaced, which shows the goddess seated on the lap of her husband in the style commonly seen in ancient [illegible]. There I secured the figure of a [illegible], about 8 inches in height, seated on a lion, and holding in her right hand a lotus and in her left a vase. These relics prove that there was a temple here, which, however, I could not trace. I also obtained from the debris of earth which I threw up from the pits I dug, some metallic relics, chiefly copper, consisting of coins, ornaments and square rings, a few diminutive [illegible] (black-[illegible]) to the eyes, and a [illegible] worn [illegible] with age.

Jamuna Dih, which is marked by the Pipra ghat [illegible], appears to be the site of a village that at first had mud huts, which accounts for the raised level of the spot, when subsequently the villagers, chiefly potters (kumhars) and potters, becoming richer during the Maurya period, built brick and tiled houses. The style of the sculpture, large bricks, and the great number of pottery and vessels, lead to this conclusion.

Sites not excavated.

I had not an opportunity to excavate at Durgah Arzani, Pahari, and the several high spots between Bankipore and the east of Patna. The Durgah where the greatest number of stone relics have been recovered, is undoubtedly one of the most promising fields; and I have the strongest reasons to look for, at the long and elevated mass of Pahari, some of the most important monuments, mentioned by the Chinese pilgrims.

CHAPTER IV. Summary of Results.

Finds grouped for three.

The results of my excavations on the sites of ancient Pataliputra may be grouped into (1) architecture, (2) sculptures, and (3) coins and minor arts. They, especially architecture, show two periods of workmanship, ancient and mediæval. By "ancient" I mean the time from Bimbisara to the end of the Maurya dynasty; and "mediæval" from the commencement of the Sunga dynasty to about 400 A.D., when the Guptas transferred their seat of government either to Ajodhya or to Kanauj, and Pataliputra began rapidly to decay. The two periods can be easily distinguished by the styles of construction and materials. Besides, the remains of the ancient period are found at a greater depth underground than those of the mediæval.

Building materials.

Wood.

The building materials of the earlier times consisted of wood, stone and bricks of the larger size than those of a later epoch. The wood, chiefly sal (Shorea robusta), was procurable in great abundance in those days, the large forests reaching northward to Vaisali, as the last journey of the Buddha from Vaisali to Kusinagara proves, as recorded in the Mahaparinibbana Sutta. Large logs of wood were brought by boats of large size down the Gandak and the Ganges. The rough blocks were cut here according to requirements, and employed in the foundations of residences, and as beams in railings, as also in palisade walls and underground drains. That the wooden posts and beams employed in residential buildings were highly carved and ornamented, will be evident to any who studies indigenous architecture in remote towns where foreign influence has not yet penetrated.

Stone.

Like the woods, the stones were also brought down here from the hills of Chunar and Rohtas in a rough-hewn state, and here they were cut and carved, according to the requirements of each edifice. The carved capital, as also a rough-hewn one of similar size, evidently intended as its duplicate, and found at Bulandi Bagh, lead to no other conclusion. Besides, at Kumrahar, I brought out from the bowels of the earth fragments of stone chips, which prove that here was at least one workshop of the ancient sculptors. The colossal pillars of the style generally associated with the name of Asoka the Great, and which I have been able to trace on the different sites, must have been brought here in a rough-hewn state, for had they been carried in an ornamented and polished state, the rough usage to which they must have been subjected on the way would have damaged the smooth surface in the transit.

Bricks.

The bricks were manufactured here, for which purpose good earth was selected, kneaded well, and moulded into the sizes of about 1 foot 8 inches long, 1 foot broad, and 3 inches thick. I cannot, however, say positively that all these bricks, undoubtedly the productions of the later period, were not manufactured here. Larger bricks were also occasionally formed, over 2 feet in length and 3 inches in thickness, for I found a fragment of very large proportions from the mounds of [illegible]. Besides, I have found several specimens of a peculiar form, being semi-cylindrical, 1 foot 6 inches in length and about 7 inches in radius, which, as Mr. [illegible], late Secretary, Public Works Department, suggested, might have served as coping of walls. Some of these semi-cylindrical forms are less in thickness and breadth than the others, being less in radius but greater in breadth. There was one from a [illegible]. Apparently in the first [illegible] these bricks have grown beautifully [illegible] with age, and it is evident that the art of preparing bricks was well understood in those days. This fact is better understood when the carved bricks, of which I have got several beautiful specimens, are seen; they show a high degree of skill and knowledge displayed by the brick-makers and potters of the Maurya period, when the Yakshas, the so-called genii of the Chinese pilgrims, were employed as masons and sculptors.

Carved bricks.

These carved bricks served as ornamental facings to walls (Plate XXXIX). One specimen, which I have got in my collection, appears to be a capital of a wall pilaster, being circular in section, with [illegible], bands and square bosses arranged diagonally to give better relief to each of the details. Another fragment exhibits the lower portion of a bas-relief, wherein the legs and lower garments of men are plainly visible. A third fragment shows another circular capital that crowned the pilaster of a temple or stupa wall. It is rather plainer in details. Some of the brick relics show fret-work and [illegible], while others have one of their edges formed into curves [illegible] of a few bricks of the same kind, or that from [illegible].

Wooden palisade and drains.

The remains of the wooden palisades and drains that I was able to find out about 20 feet below the present level of the ground, exhibit some peculiarities of construction. These beams, between 9 and

4 feet in breadth, were spread at a certain level, on which stout posts were fixed in two or four parallel rows to form the inner and outer frame-work to support the walls, floor and roof of the drain. Above the roof and at right-angles to the drain, the outer posts supported walls of thick planks to form the superstructure of the palisade. The palisade itself was, I think, constructed of two lines of plank walls, about 5 feet or more apart from each other, the intervening space being filled with earth. The superstructure being thus raised to a height of 30 feet or so, the inner wooden wall was made flush with the top of the rammed earth to form the passage for the archers or men moving under cover of the outer plank wall, which was further raised to a height of about 6 feet and was loop-holed for the discharge of arrows. This fortification wall was again strengthened by a ditch, about 200 feet wide and 30 feet deep, where the river used to flow.

The remains of ancient buildings here show that local architecture of the two periods, ancient and mediæval, embraced a variety of subjects, which may be conveniently grouped into (1) palatial and domestic, (2) ecclesiastical, and (3) monumental.

Palaces.

Of the palaces that we read of in ancient records, I have not yet been able to trace any actual remains. But an idea may easily be formed of an ancient palace from what remains in modern times, as consisting of several courts, of which the outer ones were those of [illegible] and [illegible] walls of bricks, while the royal portion had the usual Singhadwara, lion-gate, and subsidiary ones. The walls were made of stones in the lower, and bricks in the higher, portions with bastions in the corners and at intermediate distances. Some of the courts were several storeys in height, being crowned with turrets and towers and balconies. The whole palace was protected by a citadel of wooden palisade and ditches adjoining the Ganges and occupying the most prominent quarter of the city.

Of the existence of the Nil palace, where Asoka was believed to have been born, I succeeded, I think, in exposing a part on the south and west of the village of Kumrahar. Here two walls 7 feet 8 inches in thickness was found extending east to west, and having cross-walls to form rooms of rather smaller dimensions, which were communicated through narrow passages, only about 4 feet in width. Among these, steps were exposed here and there, between 5 and 7 feet below the present level of the ground. These massive walls had also a good deal of batter, in order probably to strengthen the superstructure.

Domestic architecture.

The remains of domestic architecture, which I traced at several places, and which were mostly of the mediæval period, showed thinner walls and smaller rooms,—so small indeed as to seem no better than mere cells, as those of the Nalir Palace. The walls were made of single bricks, laid lengthwise or broad. The forms of the ancient houses might be understood from the bas-reliefs on the Buddhistic railings and from the huts of ancient villages, such as Hemen. The walls were made either of brick or of earth, about one foot in thickness. The floors were also either pucca or kutcha, the pucca being made of earth, brick and lime, of which several remains I have been able to trace here. The windows were small in size and placed too high, under the eaves of the projecting gable roof, which was supported by wooden brackets, plain or ornamental, according to means of the owner. The gable roof was thatched or tiled. The tiles of those days were quite different from those now in use, being flat, not round, and having each a hole on one side to receive the knob-like point of the [illegible]. Some of the houses having gable and flat roofs were constructed, in which the lower roof was of course made flat for the [illegible]. Sometimes wooden balconies projected from the lower roof in front of the house and towards the courtyard. The gable roof had [illegible] at the vertex, [illegible] at the ends and at short intervals. A rough sketch shown will better convey an idea of the usual type of domestic architecture, which will explain the designs found in the Buddhistic railings at Budh-Gaya, Bharhut, Sanchi and other places.

Ecclesiastical architecture.

The ecclesiastical branch of ancient architecture consisted of Sangharamas (monasteries), Viharas, Chaityas and Stupas. The Vihara appears to be a chapel, enshrining some Buddhistic statues; while the stupas were memorial mounds of hemispherical form, in which relics and ashes [illegible] of the Buddha and other saints were buried in small chambers. But the term chaitya* is rather indefinite. For though in Tibet chorten means a stupa, it appears to have been employed in quite a different sense in Buddhistic and Jaina literature. The chaitya of Pavagram, where the Buddha halted, seems to be a dharmasala, while the chaityas of Vaisali, visited by him, were undoubtedly no other than temples. In Sanskrit, chaitya

* Is generally derived from Chaya = Chita, which means a funeral-pile.

[illegible] temple; so that no difference is found between vihara and chaitya. The Buddha [illegible] here was enshrined in a vihara; the Mahavana in Vaisali and the Kukkutarama vihara and the Mahabodhi temple at Bodh Gaya is known as a vihara.

Sangharamas

The Sangharamas, literally the park of the church, were extensive buildings for the Buddhist monks to live in, generally outside the city and in a shady garden. Hiuen Thsang describes the Sangharamas of old as built with extraordinary skill. "A three-storied tower is erected at each of the four angles. The beams and projecting heads are carved with great skill in different shapes. The doors, windows and the low walls are painted profusely; the monks' cells are painted inside and plain on the outside. In the very middle of the building is the hall, high and wide; there are various storied chambers and turrets of different height and shape without any fixed rule. The doors open towards the east; the royal throne also faces towards the east." (Beal's Si-yu-ki, Volume I, page 74.) Of these monastic establishments, the Chinese pilgrims mention five in Pataliputra, namely, the Mahayana, Hinayana, [illegible], and those of Upagupta and Mahendra. The Burmese records (Bigandet's Gautama) mention the convent of Vasuka, where Nagasena, the teacher and the first Buddhistic teacher of Asoka the Great lived. Besides, there were relics of several others, not particularly named by Hiuen Thsang. The Kukkutarama was somewhere east of Patna, while the Mahayana and the Hinayana were, I think, at the two Pahaŗis. I have not yet been able to explore them, nor the hill of Mahendra, which I propose to identify with the Durgah Arzani.

Viharas and stupas

Of the sites of the monumental buildings, called Vihara, only one was known to Hiuen Thsang as enshrining the footprint of the Buddha. It was most probably near the great mound of the Bari Pahari, which I propose to identify as the Great Stupa, first erected by Asoka. This stupa, as also that of the five past Buddhas, were excavated before I was deputed here. Only some brick work was cut through a depth of 40 feet or so, which almost destroyed them. Of the two stupas first erected by Asoka, which I propose to identify with the mounds of [illegible] and Jagatpura, I could not trace any remains of stone or brickwork of any importance. Only a carved architrave was found near the former of Jagatpura.

Monolithic pillars

The colossal pillars of the Maurya period prominently stand under the class of monumental architecture. I have been able to trace two of those of Pataliputra, namely, the Asoka pillar, the Nili and the [illegible], mentioned by Hiuen Thsang. I found the remains of Asoka's [illegible], and [illegible] of the north of Bhikna Pahari, Patna. I brought to light innumerable fragments of the "Lat" pillar on the north of Kumrahar, and of the pillar of the Nili Palace. I suspect [illegible] a few fragments of the latter in the west end of the village, where the main Loohan Bhawan's palace. At Kumrahar I succeeded in examining a large capital along with several fragments found below the present area of the ground. (Plate XXXIV.) Here also I found the base of another pillar of the Asoka type, but rather smaller in proportion. It is a circular stone, of which the diameter, 3 feet [illegible] inches, decreased with five steps to 2 feet 3 inches as it rose to a height of 1 foot 6 inches, and on the top of which is a circular hole about 7 feet deep, to receive the upper tenon of the shaft. The Bhikna Pahari pillar I have not yet been able to ascertain or examine. These many pillars at one place show that Pataliputra had a large share of the attention of the imperial architect.

Walls and ghats

The ghats and walls were a speciality of ancient architecture, which served the utilitarian purposes of the citizens. The existence of some large wall at Agam Kuan, of which the remains are about 20 feet, prove that others were constructed of the, if not greater, dimensions. The public wall, however, which I excavated on the north of Kumrahar, shows a peculiarity which I have not seen elsewhere. The series of the ghats, which I traced for a length of a thousand feet, is the most interesting of its kind, as proving not only the fact of the flowing of the river in the channel of the great and wide ditch of the city, but a very important feature of peculiarity of construction I have not seen in other parts of India. The stairs are small and gradually rising, built horizontal and vertical layers of bricks, and finished and strengthened by [illegible] in the [illegible] [illegible], while three longitudinal walls, one rising over the other at short distances, encase them in a whole.

Buddhist railings

Few traces of the so-called Buddhist railings have been found in course of explorations, the most at the Durgah Arzani, the third at Kumrahar, and the [illegible] in the north-west of the Bulandi Bagh. (Plate XL, [illegible], [illegible], XLIII.) The first is of very plain style, there is a plain [illegible], one having posts and horizontal bars without any ornament. I found three of it, of which the height was about 3 feet 6 inches. The second railing, found at Durgah Arzani, had smaller posts, which were carved on the front face with half circles at top and bottom, and a full one in the middle, while the edges between them were bevelled. The central ones show some carvings of tigers and other animals. The horizontal bars, which were fixed to the posts, were not segmental in section, as is generally seen in these railings, but rectangular, being two to three feet, not three, as generally is the case. These three bars, rectangular in section, were fixed, not in the centre of the side face, but very close to the carved front, a peculiarity which I have not seen elsewhere. This fact shows that the Durgah railing was attached to a brick wall or either a [illegible] or a stage, half the posts being embedded in the masonry work, as shown in the sketch. The third railing, of which two posts and two fragments of the horizontal bars were discovered and secured by me at Kumrahar, is the most ornate of the three. The posts possess the usual embellishments of the two semi-circles, at the top and bottom, which are adorned with lotus flowers, and in the middle the circular lotus, while at the sides were the three parallel bars, segmental in section, of which the centre had such a lotus, relieved with figures. The central lotus of the two posts has reliefs in circular compartments, one being a group of dancing husband and wife, the other [illegible], and having [illegible]. The other group is a seated gentleman, whose [illegible] two children at his sides. A fragment of a coping-stone, most probably belonging to this railing, has now been found here; it shows two trees of the conventional type, three standing men and three [illegible]. There are on the outer surface two holes, about two feet from each other, to let in the tenons of the posts underneath. These railings are generally called Buddhistic, since the time when Fergusson gave that name to them, but as they are found throughout India, I have not yet found sufficient reason to say that they were exclusively Buddhistic and not generally Hindu.

Ancient sculpture.

The relics of ancient sculpture, both Brahmanical and Buddhistic, are several, being generally collected and worshipped near the modern temples of Patna and Bankipore. (Plates LIII, LIV, LV.) The Brahmanical statues consist of Surya, sun-god, [illegible], Vishnu, Parvati, Ganesa, &c. The Buddhistic figures, which are not so many as the Brahmanical ones, are the sitting images, Buddhas, Padmapanis, Tara and Mayadevi. The pretty large [illegible] having four faces on its four sides, and a large Surya, [illegible] in the middle, with other [illegible], are in the temple of Choti Patan Devi. Near the temple, in the compound of the civil court and under a tree, are two votive stones, carved in the model of a temple, of which each side contains a figure.

The winged lion, of which I have found three, shows the most ancient style of sculpture, generally associated with the Maurya period. (Plate XLVI.) The [illegible] now worshipped as [illegible] Devi at [illegible], and found some 40 years ago on the west side of the village of [illegible], must have belonged to the same period, the pose being very graceful and the details showing interesting features of the indigenous art. (Plate L.) But the most important relics of the ancient sculpture are now in the Calcutta Museum, where they were removed at the end of the last century. (Plate LI.) They appear to be two Yaksha guards, about 6 feet in height and [illegible] of the earliest art, the [illegible] and [illegible] of the drapery and the folds of their dress being very well shown. They are inscribed with names in the ancient Pali characters, as Yakha [illegible] and [illegible], or something like them. They were found outside the city of Patna.

At the Durgah Arzani were found several relics of ancient sculpture, of which a [illegible], showing [illegible], is the most interesting. (Plate XLIV.) There were also found, imbedded in the walls, two figures, one a goddess and the other a male standing figure, which appeared to be of the early Gupta period. (Plates LI, LII.) Here also is an elaborately ornamented pillar, of which the top and bottom are square in section, and octagonal and sixteen-sided in the intervening spaces of the shaft, which the Mahomedans utilised as a head-stone or rather lamp-post to a [illegible] grave on a mound which was hollowed out in the middle for the lamp to be set in. (Plate XLVI.) It has some inscriptions in shell characters on two faces, (see Plate XLVI for an impression.)

Pottery.

Ancient pottery is represented here by several kinds of specimens. (Plate LVI.) The carved bricks have been mentioned already. The vases and vessels, found in the excavations, display graceful forms of different shapes, which are now forgotten by modern potters [illegible]. One peculiar vessel, shaped like a bell, has several [illegible] at the bottom, and the intervening spaces are ornamented with [illegible]. One jar, [illegible], was found at Kumrahar. Some [illegible] show [illegible]. Of terracotta figures, I have [illegible] from the [illegible], having dress and ornaments peculiar to the age.

Coins.

Though the number of ancient coins found in my excavations is not very large, still they show a variety of style and are valuable as regards the history of the city. (Plate LVII.) They range from the punch-marked to that of the Gupta. The one of the [illegible], which was mostly found in the excavations at Kumrahar, is generally rectangular, one being very large and almost square. The symbols in them are the wheel, [illegible], and many indistinguishable signs. The tree and elephant type are rather large and circular in size, having a [illegible] on one side and a tree (bodhidruma) on the reverse, with some subsidiary signs as well. The Chaitya and elephant class is smaller and square, having the sign of a so-called Chaitya on one face and an elephant on the other. Of the two Gupta coins, one found at Kumrahar is of the [illegible] type, having [illegible] the upper half of the figure of Chandra Gupta II, and on the reverse a [illegible], underneath which was the legend, now defaced with age. The other Gupta coin belongs to the same king, showing only the head, and being smaller in size. All these coins are of copper; only one punch-marked was found [illegible]. A Chinese coin was also discovered along with two punch-marked coins at Bulandibagh. It is circular in shape, having a [illegible] in the centre.

Beads.—I have found in my excavations a number of ancient beads, many of which are very interesting as showing variegated colours and forms. Some are round, some oval, and a few cylindrical. A very few of them possess a marking in the middle of one of the longer sides. Many of them have lost their polish through age. One large but broken bead, a portion of a [illegible] is still shining. The beautiful blending and contrasts of the colours are particularly noted by those who see them.

Beads.

The specimens of ironwork in nails and [illegible] show that the forms now used are not much different from those of ancient types (Plate LVIII.). The large nails are mostly of the shape now in use. One crowbar that I have got in my collection is the most worn in its original shape. It is a long piece, having a [illegible] at the lower end. I have another piece [illegible] end.

Iron [illegible].

In the excavation on the eastern ditch of [illegible], and while [illegible] the wooden [illegible], a peculiar ornament, most probably belonging to a [illegible], was brought to light. It was gilded with golden leaves (Plate LVII.). The details are pretty; at one end of the cylindrical form is a knob in the centre, which is surrounded by what appear to be petals of a lotus flower projecting at the edges. The cylindrical [illegible] narrow in the middle, relieved with [illegible] and very gracefully; while the other end is rather plain and narrow [illegible] the ornament to the [illegible] of the [illegible]. The construction of the ornament is not clearly understood, being of unknown workmanship of some kind of [illegible]. I have also got some copper rings* and studs [illegible] and some pieces of ornaments (Plate LVII.).

* [illegible]

That the artisans of the Maurya period also [illegible] a high degree of skill is proved by their workmanship in [illegible], in which they [illegible] beads, vessels and ornaments. In [illegible] such as the spotted [illegible] from the beds of hilly streams, [illegible] articles were manufactured. A [illegible] but pretty one in stone was found in the excavations for palisade at [illegible]. Another ornament, probably of [illegible], was [illegible]. A large circular piece about 3 inches in diameter [illegible] of which the edge [illegible], also a piece of [illegible] were also found in the [illegible] where the Maurya pillar was detected.

Judging my collection of ancient relics as a whole, it will be seen that the results of archaeological researches and excavations have proved [illegible]. Though I have not yet been successful in discovering any inscription, I doubt not that future excavations will bring to light many relics of the [illegible]. Palisades existed between [illegible] and [illegible] feet below our feet, and the remains of the [illegible] of the Maurya Empire are all buried [illegible] beads, jewels, and [illegible] being [illegible] by [illegible] earth, till an excavator like me will bring them to light, to the surprise of the learned and the [illegible].

Results [illegible].

Conclusion, and promising sites recommended for further excavations.

From what I have detailed in the foregoing chapters, [illegible] that the two Palaces are the most promising sites for excavation, for here I hope to find an inscribed pillar, the [illegible], and the two monasteries, besides the relics of the two Stupas already identified by me.

Two Palaces.

Kumrahar and its neighbourhood [illegible] be further explored for the [illegible] palace and another inscribed pillar. The [illegible] pillar should [illegible] beyond the depth I [illegible] last year.

Kumrahar.

Bahadurpur and Rampur [illegible] the attention of the archaeological [illegible] in order to examine further the extensive [illegible] remains discovered by Mr. Mills and myself.

Bahadurpur, Rampur.

[illegible] is the most important place for the [illegible] palisade, the Asoka pillar, and [illegible], a mine of archaeological [illegible].

[illegible]

[illegible] the very interesting [illegible] of [illegible] remains [illegible].

The Tangah Arrak, [illegible] the greatest number of [illegible] appears to be a [illegible] site, and I doubt not that important [illegible] will be [illegible] the [illegible] is explored [illegible].

Tangah Arrak.

The [illegible] palisade of [illegible] will [illegible] to be [illegible]. Though I have [illegible] the lines of the city and traced the palisade from [illegible], Bahadurpur, and [illegible] to Mangal Talao, [illegible] to be determined.

Palisade.

[illegible] city and [illegible] the [illegible] pillar, [illegible] should be opened and examined by all means, while the [illegible] probably the site of the Maurya city palace, should be explored.

[illegible]

And last not, but not the least of the ancient monuments is the Kukkutarama monastery, where the third Buddhistic council was held in [illegible] (B.C.), should be sought for on the south-east of Patna.

Kukkutarama.

These important sites will convey an idea of the amount of explorations required for the proper understanding of what was the nature of the grand capital of the Mauryan Empire and the position it occupied in the history of ancient India. All these works cannot be done in one year, considering the limited sum sanctioned for them.

Further exploration in [illegible] season.

P. C. Mukharji,

Archaeologist.

Bankipore,

The [illegible] March [illegible].

www.ingramcontent.com/pod-product-compliance
Lightning Source LLC
Chambersburg PA
CBHW032142080426
42733CB00008B/1167

* 9 7 8 3 3 3 7 3 8 4 8 1 4 *